D1634513

# Palace Architecture

## Southwestern View of the Hall of Supreme Harmony

preceding page

The Hall of Supreme Harmony is not only the largest hall in the Forbidden City, but also the largest extant wood structure in China. The hall was built in 1420, or the 18th year in the Yongle reign of Ming Emperor Chengzu. The structure was repeatedly destroyed by fire in intervening years and was rebuilt during the 34th year of the Kangxi reign of Qing Emperor Shizu. The ornate Hall of Supreme Harmony sits on a three-tiered marble terrace rising eight m in height. A Jialiang (a bronze standard grain measure housed in a pavilion-like stone stand) and a stone sundial on the terrace symbolize the balance of power under heaven. The expansive courtyard and three-tiered terrace stress the supreme position of the hall, and implies the total supremacy of the emperor.

The Excellence of Ancient Chinese Architecture

# PALACE ARCHITECTURE

## Imperial Palaces of the Last Dynasty

Ru Jinghua
Peng Hualiang

China Architecture & Building Press

# Map of Historic Sites of Capital Cities and Palaces

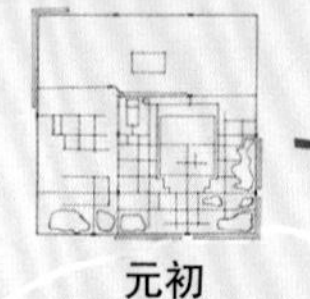

元初
上都城址平面图
Early Yuan, Plan of the Site of the Upper Capital

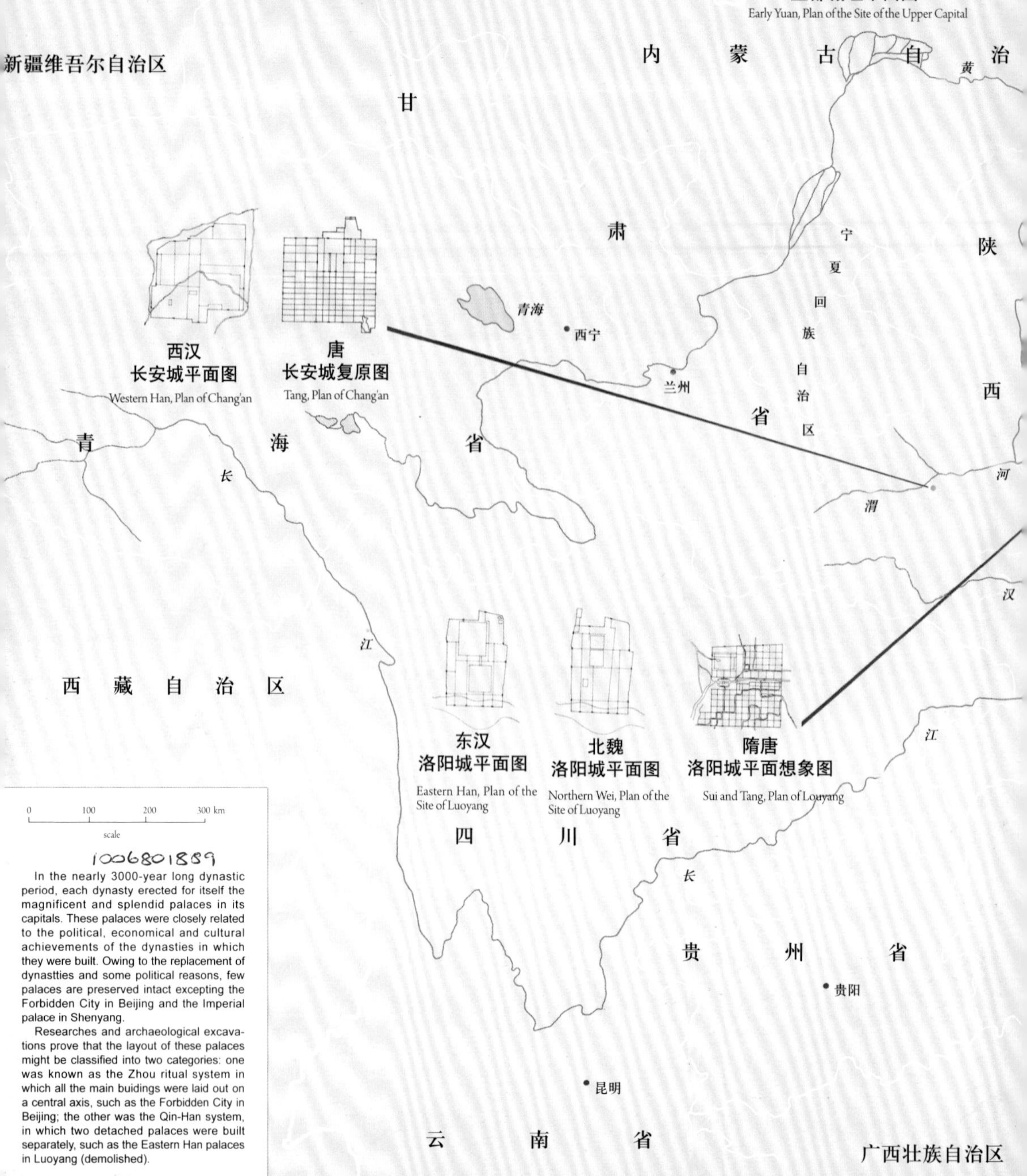


西汉
长安城平面图
Western Han, Plan of Chang'an

唐
长安城复原图
Tang, Plan of Chang'an

东汉
洛阳城平面图
Eastern Han, Plan of the Site of Luoyang

北魏
洛阳城平面图
Northern Wei, Plan of the Site of Luoyang

隋唐
洛阳城平面想象图
Sui and Tang, Plan of Louyang



In the nearly 3000-year long dynastic period, each dynasty erected for itself the magnificent and splendid palaces in its capitals. These palaces were closely related to the political, economical and cultural achievements of the dynasties in which they were built. Owing to the replacement of dynastties and some political reasons, few palaces are preserved intact excepting the Forbidden City in Beijing and the Imperial palace in Shenyang.

Researches and archaeological excavations prove that the layout of these palaces might be classified into two categories: one was known as the Zhou ritual system in which all the main buidings were laid out on a central axis, such as the Forbidden City in Beijing; the other was the Qin-Han system, in which two detached palaces were built separately, such as the Eastern Han palaces in Luoyang (demolished).

吉 林 省
清初
盛京都城平面图
Early Qing, Plan of the Imperial Palace in Prosperous Capital
沈阳 Shenyang
辽 宁 省
正蓝旗（敦达浩特）
Blue Banner (Dundahot)
Beijing
北京市
天津市
渤 海
金
中都平面示意图
Jin, Plan of Zhongdu
元
大都平面想象图
Yuan, Plan of the Site of Dadu
明
北京城平面图
Ming, Plan of Beijing
清
北京城平面图
Qing, Plan of Beijing
河 北
山 西 省
太原市
石家庄
济南
山 东 省
黄
临漳
Linzhang
曹魏
邺城平面想象图
Wei of the Three Kingdoms, Plan of Yecheng
海
洛阳
偃师 Yanshi
Kaifeng
开封
河 南 省
江 苏 省
Fengyang
凤阳
安 徽
合肥
南京
Nanjing
上海市
杭州
东晋、南朝
建康平面想象图
Eastern Jin and Southern Dynasties, Plan of Jiankang
明初
南京城平面图
Early Ming, Plan of Nanjing
湖 北 省
浙 江 省
湖 南
江 西 省
商
二里头
一号宫殿遗址平面图
Shang, Plan of the Ruins of Erlitou Palace No. 1
北宋
东京平面想象图
Northern Song, Plan of Eastern Capital (Bianliang)
明初
中都城址平面图
Early Ming, Plan of the Site Zhongdu
福州
台北
福 建 省
台 湾 海 陕
台 湾 省
广 东 省
广州

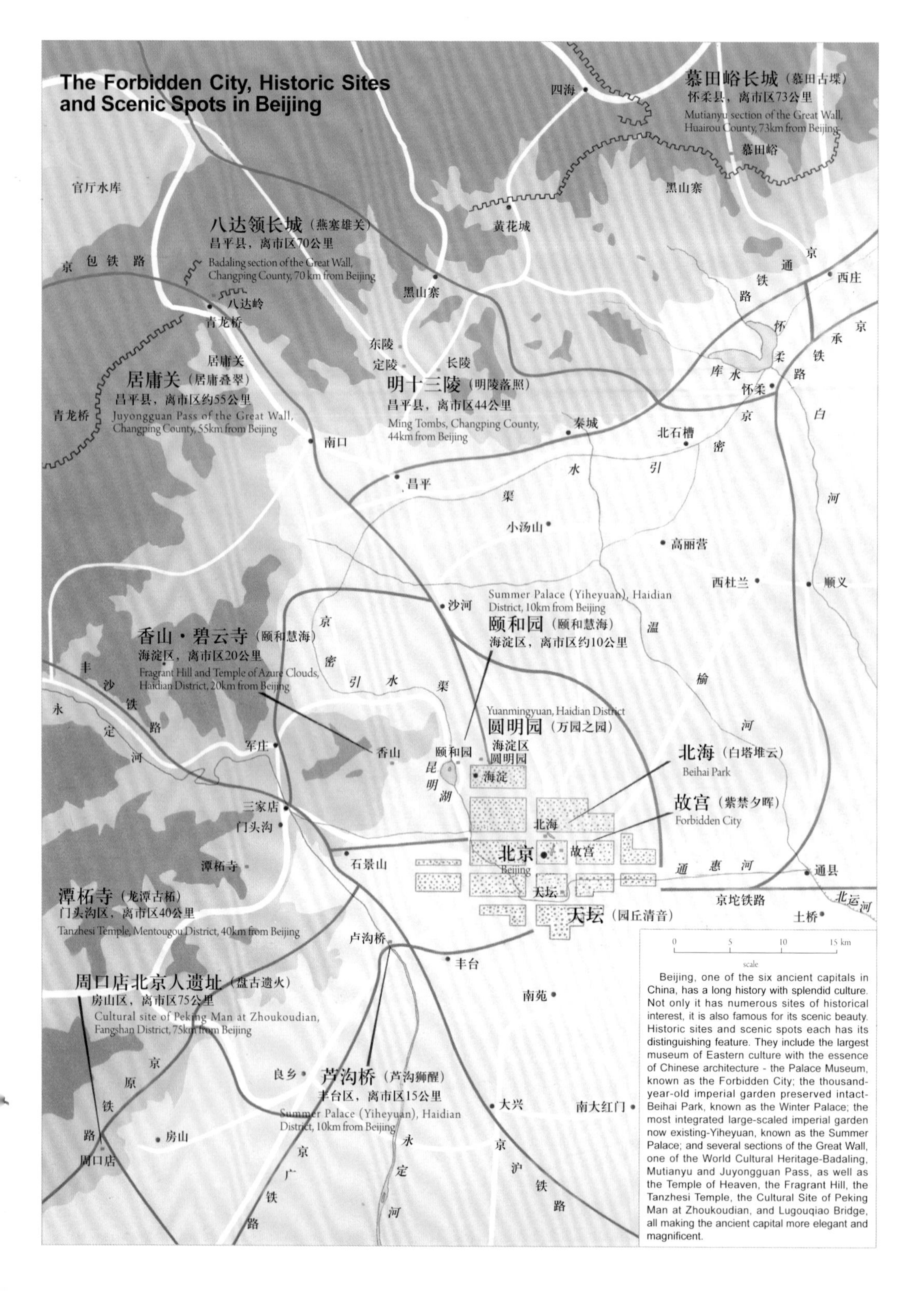
The Forbidden City, Historic Sites
and Scenic Spots in Beijing
慕田峪长城（慕田古堞）
怀柔县，离市区73公里
Mutianyu section of the Great Wall,
Huairou County, 73km from Beijing
四海
慕田峪
黑山寨
官厅水库
黄花城
八达领长城（燕塞雄关）
昌平县，离市区70公里
Badaling section of the Great Wall,
Changping County, 70 km from Beijing
京包铁路
八达岭
青龙桥
黑山寨
京通铁路
西庄
怀柔水库
京承铁路
东陵
定陵
长陵
居庸关
居庸关（居庸叠翠）
昌平县，离市区约55公里
Juyongguan Pass of the Great Wall,
Changping County, 55km from Beijing
明十三陵（明陵落照）
昌平县，离市区44公里
Ming Tombs, Changping County,
44km from Beijing
青龙桥
怀柔
秦城
京密引水渠
北石槽
白河
南口
昌平
小汤山
高丽营
西杜兰
顺义
沙河
Summer Palace (Yiheyuan), Haidian
District, 10km from Beijing
颐和园（颐和慧海）
海淀区，离市区约10公里
香山·碧云寺（颐和慧海）
海淀区，离市区20公里
Fragrant Hill and Temple of Azure Clouds,
Haidian District, 20km from Beijing
京密引水渠
温榆河
丰沙铁路
永定河
Yuanmingyuan, Haidian District
圆明园（万园之园）
军庄
香山
颐和园
海淀区
圆明园
北海（白塔堆云）
Beihai Park
昆明湖
海淀
三家店
门头沟
北海
故宫（紫禁夕晖）
Forbidden City
北京
Beijing
故宫
潭柘寺
石景山
通惠河
通县
天坛
京坨铁路
北运河
潭柘寺（龙潭古柘）
门头沟区，离市区40公里
Tanzhesi Temple, Mentougou District, 40km from Beijing
天坛（园丘清音）
土桥
卢沟桥
丰台
0 5 10 15 km
scale
周口店北京人遗址（盘古遗火）
房山区，离市区75公里
Cultural site of Peking Man at Zhoukoudian,
Fangshan District, 75km from Beijing
南苑
京原铁路
良乡
芦沟桥（芦沟狮醒）
丰台区，离市区15公里
Summer Palace (Yiheyuan), Haidian
District, 10km from Beijing
大兴
南大红门
房山
周口店
京广铁路
永定河
京沪铁路
Beijing, one of the six ancient capitals in China, has a long history with splendid culture. Not only it has numerous sites of historical interest, it is also famous for its scenic beauty. Historic sites and scenic spots each has its distinguishing feature. They include the largest museum of Eastern culture with the essence of Chinese architecture - the Palace Museum, known as the Forbidden City; the thousand-year-old imperial garden preserved intact-Beihai Park, known as the Winter Palace; the most integrated large-scaled imperial garden now existing-Yiheyuan, known as the Summer Palace; and several sections of the Great Wall, one of the World Cultural Heritage-Badaling, Mutianyu and Juyongguan Pass, as well as the Temple of Heaven, the Fragrant Hill, the Tanzhesi Temple, the Cultural Site of Peking Man at Zhoukoudian, and Lugouqiao Bridge, all making the ancient capital more elegant and magnificent.

# Contents

## Notes on the Photographs

### The Forbidden City in Beijing

**The Imperial Palace in Shenyang**

## Appendices

## Editor's Note

- The series consists of ten volumes, each of which deals with respectively palace architecture, imperial mausoleums, imperial gardens, private gardens, vernacular dwellings, Buddhist buildings, Taoist buildings, Islamic buildings, ritual and ceremonious buildings and defense structures..
- Each volume is basically composed of four sections, i.e. general introduction, colour photographs, glossary and chronology of major events.
- The general introduction describes the background, development process, architectural characteristics of different types of buildings and is complimented with photographs and drawings.
- The colour photographs are arranged in the order of building distribution area or the time when the building was completed. The series contains about 1,700 exquisite colour photographs, which are attached with captions explaining the location, construction time, and artistic and technical features.
- Each volume is accompanied with layout plan, drawing of recovered buildings, distribution map and travel guide to mark the location of famous buildings and cultural attractions in the vicinity.
- The glossary is arrayed according to the sequence of strokes of Chinese characters, which is a reference for general readers.
- Chronology of major events is affiliated with each volume of the series. Chinese traditional chronology is adopted in the annals of the series, and is also indicated in the Christian era for easy reference.

# Preface 1

China enjoys a long and profound history of ancient architecture. Her verifiable artifacts could be dated back to 7,000 years ago from Hemudu ruins in Yuyao to Banpo ruins in Xi'an. Of course, architecture underwent a long process from primitiveness to sophistication before the Warring States, while in the Qin and Han dynasties, it gained an apparent progress along with the development of production and unification of the country. Moreover, in over a thousand years of the prosperous Tang Dynasty to the Ming and Qing dynasties, it reached several unprecedented peaks which were embodied by diversified building forms and refined planning and exquisite construction.

The love of architecture is the love of history and culture. China Architecture & Building Press (CABP), from the very beginning of its founding, has defined the sorting out and publication of traditional Chinese architecture and the enhancement of Chinese culture as one of important themes in its mission. In 1950s and 1960s, many monographs on the subject by experts such as Liang Sicheng, Liu Dunzhen, Tong Jun, Liu Zhiping and others were published. In early 1980s when China was just opened to the outside world, CABP set aside a special fund for publication of academic books on ancient Chinese architecture despite of the limited financial capability then. As a result, large academic albums of Ancient *Chinese Architecture, Ancient Architecture in Chengde, the Art of Chinese Gardens, the Buildings of Confucius Temple in Qufu, Ancient Buildings of Putuoshan, Summer Palace as well as* five volumes of *History of Ancient Chinese Architecture* were put forth continuously. Those books have proved to be of high academic and practical values in consolidation, conservation and protection of the national treasure.

*The Excellence of Ancient Chinese Architecture* in English is a series of ten volumes on various aspects of the ancient Chinese architecture, which offer a comprehensive coverage of the art, highlighted by the supreme quality of the photos as well as plenty of drawings of plans, sections and perspectives. The easy description would lead to a comprehension of the cultural essence of Chinese architecture, and appreciation of the aesthetics and philosophy embodied by the art. The authors are famous Chinese experts who have long been engaged in the study of the related subjects, whose dedication makes the series authoritative and informative for interested laymen and specialists alike. Now the Excellence of Ancient Chinese Architecture is published. It is a happy event. I believe that it will serve as a door for all those who are interested in the study of ancient Chinese architecture.

**Zhou Yi**

Former President
China Architecture & Building Press

Former Chairman, Committee on Publication of Science Books
Vice Chairman, Chinese Association of Publishers

# Preface 2

As history advances in the new era of the 21st century, China is once again becoming the focus of worldwide attention. The rich variety of her landscape, the wisdom of her people, the current unprecedented economic growth, and the wealth of her cultural heritage are all becoming the subject of worldwide interest.

In China's extensive and profound cultural treasury, ancient architecture is one of the important components, which, in a sense, is of a symbolic nature. The beauty and elegance of ancient Chinese architecture has a uniqueness of its own in the world architectural system. The strict formality of the city layouts, the lively arrangement of village settlements, the grouping of buildings around courtyards, the comprehensive building code for wood structures, the great variety of colour and architectural form, the perfect harmony of the decorative and structural functions of building elements, the integration of furniture, interior decoration, painting, sculpture and calligraphy into a comprehensive art of architecture, all go to manifest the distinctive characteristics of the traditional Chinese culture. A perusal of the country's magnificent palaces and temples, her tranquil and intricate gardens, the wide variety of her vernacular dwellings, and the exquisiteness of her pavilions and roofed walkways, will lead to a better understanding of China and her people. When one comes to study China's ancient architecture, he will have a deeper comprehension of the oriental philosophy of the "oneness of nature and man" inherent in the architectural forms, as well as of the Chinese people's respect for Confucianism, the expression of their philosophical meditation on time and space through material forms, and their all-embracing aesthetic tastes.

Now the *Excellence of Ancient Chinese Architecture* is published. I believe the vivid and colourful photos will render our readers an enjoyment of aesthetics, and the easy descriptions will facilitate our readers in understanding the cultural essence of ancient Chinese architecture. Under the trend of globalization, it will surely promote the academic exchange internationally and deepen the cultural cooperation among different peoples of the world.

**Ye Rutang** | Former Vice Minister
Ministry of Construction

The Excellence of Ancient Chinese Architecture

# Palace Architecture

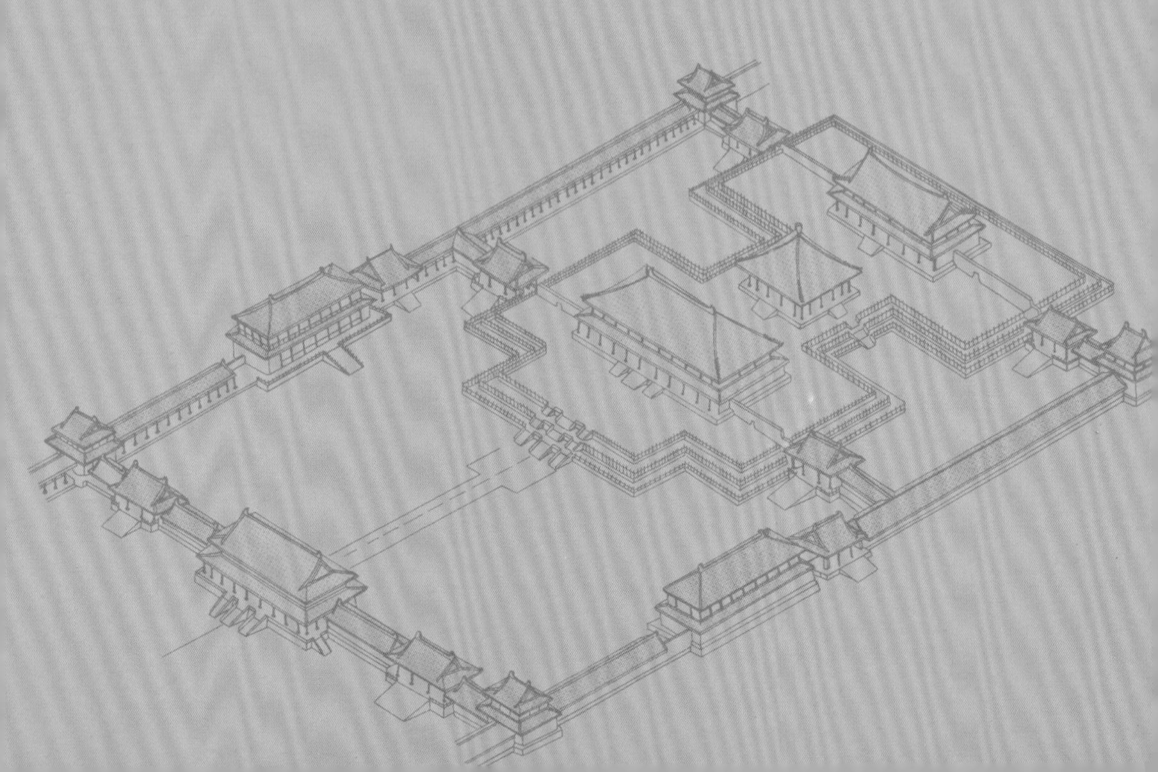

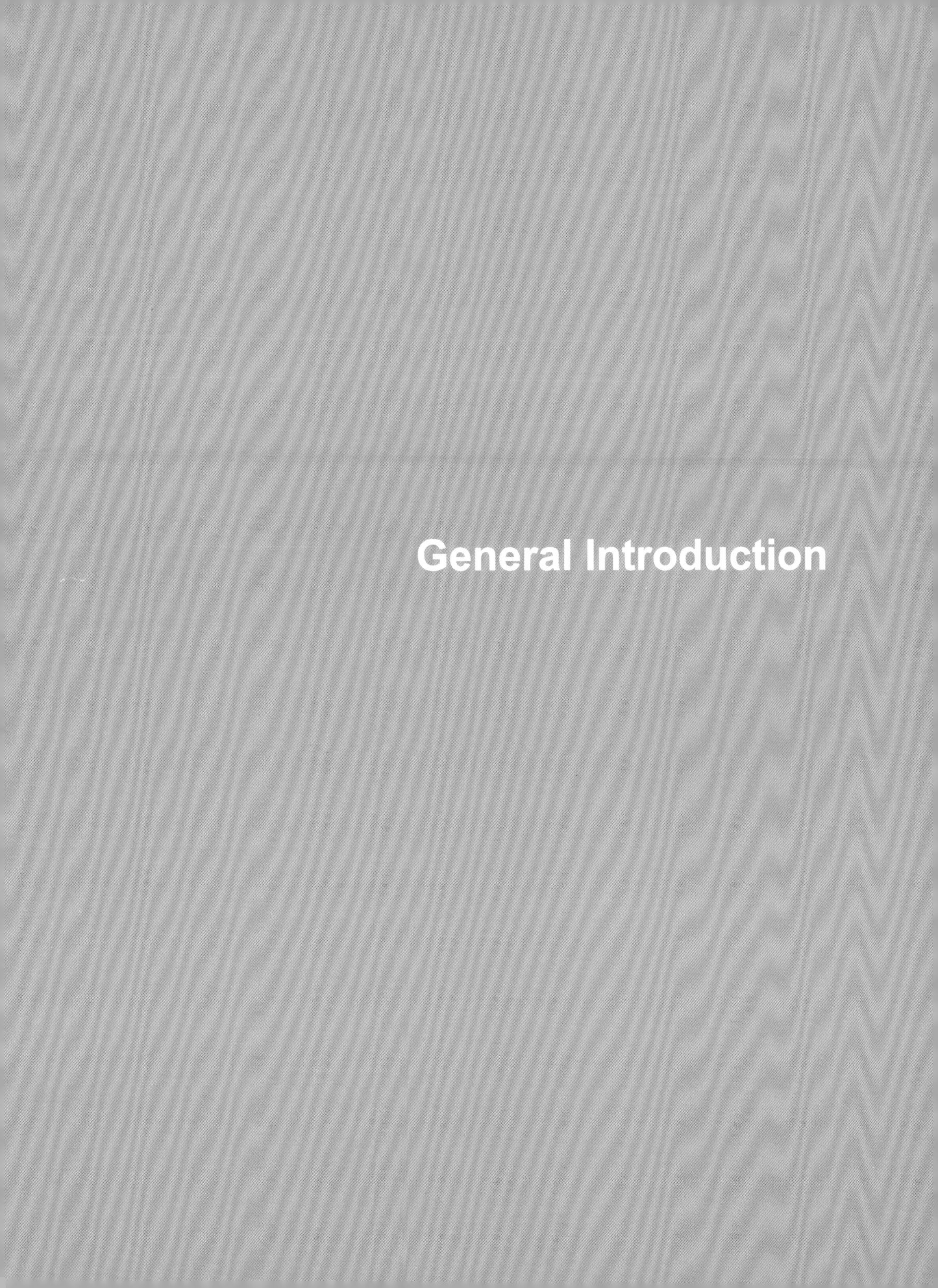

# General Introduction

# Historical Records on Palace Architecture

## —— From Primitive Crude Houses to Magnificent Buildings

Examination of ancient literature and documents reveals many historical records on palace architecture.

One of the earliest is in *the Book of Changes* (Yi Jing), which notes that in the earliest times, people did not live in houses, and even the rulers were not aware of what houses were. In winter, people lived in caves and in summer, wood-piled nests. Undoubtedly, there were no special terms or words for the ruler's residence, or the palaces. It was not until the Shang Dynasty (c.16th~11th century BC), that there really appeared two characters inscribed on oracle bones which meant houses for human beings to live in. As time went on, and the society forged ahead, along with the establishment of the empire and the appearance of a dynastic system of emperors, the meaning of these two characters was narrowed only to refer to the emperor's residence, or the imperial palace, where the emperor lived, conducted state affairs, summoned meetings and held ceremonies to meet the needs of the monarchical and patriarchal-feudal system. Thereafter, palaces progressively constituted a special type of architecture.

### I. The Primitive Phase

A building site discovered and excavated at Erlitou Village in Yanshi County, Henan Province, is considered part of a primitive dynastic palace, built around 1900~1500 BC, i.e., in the late Xia or the early Shang Dynasty. The site, as it now appears, is a large rammed-earth terrace, several dozen centim in height and nearly square in plan. Each side of the terrace is over a hundred m long. According to the unearthed post holes and dilapidated walls, it was thought the site was the ruins of a courtyard enclosed with covered walks on all four sides. A gateway to the courtyard was located in the middle of the southern flank. In the centre of the courtyard, there used to be a south-facing, eight-bay palatial hall, with its length from east to west over 30 m and its depth from south to north more than 10 m. In the light of ancient literature, a palatial hall

**A Bird's-eye View of the Forbidden City**

During the Ming Dynasty, the Forbidden City was built in the centre of the capital, with a layout according to the rule:" to place the Ancestral Temple on the left, the Altar of Land and Grain on the right, the Court in the front and the market in the rear", thus forming an example most closely following the layout of the capital of the Zhou Dynasty recorded in the Survey on Construction Work in the Ritual of Zhou. Since the Manchus entered the area inside the Shanhaiguan Pass and seized the state power in Beijing, the Forbidden City continued to be used by the Qing Court. It underwent restoration and extension several times, but the general layout remains intact. The Forbidden City measures 961 m from north to south and 753 m from east to west, with a total area of 720,000 $m^2$.

of the Shang Dynasty like this should be a hip-roofed, wood-framed building with eaves double-tiered and thatched roofing. This should be a typical building complex at that time, i.e., a courtyard with the main hall in the centre and covered walks all around. Though the layout and construction method were in primitive phase, their traces may still be found, to some extent, in the Forbidden City of the Ming-Qing periods.

Certain ritual buildings, with an integrated ritualistic system, were said to have existed in the Zhou Dynasty. *The Survey on Construction Work* (Kao Gong Ji) collected in *the Ritual of Zhou* (Zhou Li), written around the Spring and Autumn and the Warring States Periods, records the planning principles of the Zhou capital. The walled palatial complex is the main part, inside of which are three gates and three halls, arranged in proper order to meet the needs of the outer and the inner courts. Outside, there is the Ancestral Temple on the left, and the Altar of Land and Grain on the right. These principles have not been reflected evidently in the Qin and the Han capitals, but their influence has grown stronger and stronger in the later dynasties.

## II. Rise of the Imperial Palace

The State of Qin annexed the six other states and founded a centralized autocratic feudal empire, China's first, in 221 BC. The term Huang Di was created to refer to the emperor. Qin Shi Huang Di, or the first emperor of the Qin Dynasty, built his palaces on a vast scale. Palatial buildings were erected at more than 140 places in the northern suburbs of the capital, Xianyang. All were built in styles to imitate the palatial buildings of each of the six conquered states. Over ten thousand beauties were kept in these buildings. Shi Huang Di further enlarged the scale of construction. He was planning to build another palatial complex in Shanglin Garden to the south of the Wei River. According to the records in the Basic Annals of Qin Shi Huang, *in Records of the History* (Shi Ji), he built the front hall Epang or Efanggong first. Since the empire came

**Zhaochen Building Sites of the Western Zhou Dynasty**

Since 1976, archaeological investigations have been carried out in the area around Zhouyuan. Fifteen building remains within an area of 5,000 $m^2$ were discovered in Zhaochen village, Fuleng County. Foundations of round columns made of rammed earth with gravel mixed were unearthed.

**Site of Epang (or Efanggong) Palace of the Qin Dynasty**

In 21 BC, in the 35th year of his reign, Qin Shi Huang Di, the first Emperor, built a palatial complex called Zhao Gong, of which Epang or Efanggong was the front hall. When the Second Emperor ascended the throne, the construction of epang was held up for the construction of the mausoleum of the First Emperor. A year later when the construction of Epang was resumed, the original plan had been reduced. When the Qin Dynasty was overthrown, construction had not been completed.

into existence, the character 宫(gong) was used only to mean the imperial palace or palatial complex, while the character 殿(dian) was used for the palatial hall. Later, the two characters 宫殿 were combined to represent palace in a general sense.

In the Qin Dynasty, there used to be a great number of palatial complexes scattered all over the vast areas to the north and south of the Wei River, and linked by paved roads or elevated ways. Unfortunately, when the front hall Epang or Efangong was still under construction, the emperor died. Later on, rebels led by Xiang Yu burned down all the Qin palaces, and the fires lasted for more than three months. Now, in the site of Epang palace, there remains a big rammed-earth terrace, rectangular in plan, with its east-west length of about 1000 m and north-south width of about 500 m. Some eave-tiles (tile ends) have been discovered there.

The site of the Qin capital Xianyang, is situated in the eastern suburbs of today's Xianyang city, Shaanxi Province. Indeed, many palatial building remains can still be found there, along with some rammed-earth belts linking them. These are regarded as the foundations of the paved roads or storied covered walks among the palaces.

## III. Weiyang Palace

At the beginning of the establishment of the Han Dynasty, the emperor Liu Bang did not build a new palace. He only extended a Qin palace in the southern suburbs of Xianyang. He renamed it Changle Palace (Palace of Everlasting Happiness). Later, when he returned to the capital, Chang'an, from an expedition, he found a new building called Weiyang Palace (Palace of Ended-Not-Yet) being built under the supervision of Xiao He, one of his higher officials. He asked why Xiao had built such a luxurious palace. Xiao replied: "Your Majesty is the Son of Heaven, You should make yourself home wherever you are. You should build your palace as magnificent as it can be. Otherwise, it is hard to show the world how majestic and dignified an emperor is." When the Palace was completed in the next year, Liu Bang gave his officials and officers a grand entertainment in the front hall of the palace. Then, he was pleased by the cheers of "Long live Your Majesty!" Others followed, such as the Northern Palace, Palace of Osmanthus, Palace of Brilliance, and the city wall of Chang'an was progressively formed after they were completed. Chang'an is in the northwest of today's city of Xi'an.

**A Restoration Drawing of the Hall of Universal Origins in Daming Palace of the Tang Dynasty**

The Hall of Universal Origins was the main hall in Daming Palace of the Tang Dynasty. It was built on the top of the Dragon Head Hill, which was made as the high terrace of the main hall. The existent site measures some 10 m high. Excavations demonstrate that the hall has 11 bays with a 75-metre-long imperial way, called the Dragon-Tail Way, in front, and there were two pavilions located on either wing, linked by galleries with L-shaped plan to the Hall of Universal Origins.

Archaeological excavations of the ancient capital in the past few decades have revealed that the site of the Weiyang Palace is square in plan, enclosed by walls, 2,150 m from east to west and 2,250 m from north to south.

## IV. Daming Palace

The Tang Dynasty (618~906 AD) introduced a period of extraordinary vigor and prosperity. It was also a mature period of Chinese architecture, which exerted a tremendous influence upon the neighboring countries. The Tang capital Chang'an, situated to the southwest of the Han capital, was the largest city in the world at that time, with an area of 84 $km^2$, 9,721 m from east to west by 8,651 m from north to south. Its area was ten times of that of the city Xi'an of the Ming Dynasty. The Palatial City was rectangular in plan. Inside, there were the Supreme Ultimate Palace (Taiji Gong), the Eastern Palace and the Yeting Palace, where the emperor, princes and the imperial family lived their daily life respectively.

The Tang Emperor Gaozong suffered from serious rheumatism and disliked the dampness of the low-lying Supreme Ultimate Palace. So, he built Daming Palace (Palace of Grand Brightness) on the Dragon Head Plain, a highland area outside the northern city wall. Since then, Daming Palace was used for the emperor to live in and conduct state affairs permanently. Excavations on the site of Daming Palace proved that the palatial city walls were built of rammed earth, partly faced with bricks. Its northern wall was 1,135 m long; the southern wall, 1,670 m and the western wall, 2,256 m. Its eastern wall linked up the eastern ends of the southern and the northern walls, although not perpendicular to either of them. To the due north of the south gate of Daming Palace, were the Hanyuandian (Hall of Universal Origins), Xuanzhengdian (Hall of State Affairs) and Zichendian (Hall of Purple Polaris) on the new axial line. To the east and west of this line, there were halls and pavilions placed symmetrically. In the rear were the living halls for the emperor and empress, as well as the imperial family. At the rear was the imperial garden, comprising the Imperial Lake, Hill of Immortals and other landscaped buildings.

The 11-bay Hanyuandian was the main hall of Daming Palace. All that remains now are a terrace, ten-odd m high, east-west 76 m in length and south-north 42 m in width. Archaeological excavations prove that there used to be two pavilions, Xiangluange and Qifengge, standing ahead to the left and to the right of the main hall. The pavilions and the main hall were linked by galleries, forming a large, U-shaped palatial complex, which was, to some extent, similar to the plan of the Meridian Gate of the Forbidden City in Beijing. There were seven flights of steps 75 m long from the ground straight up to the main hall. The uppermost flight was much steeper than the lower ones. The imperial way with the flight of steps was paved with clay tiles engraved with lotus motif. Stone balustrades were placed in rows on either side. It looked like a dragon tail at a distance, so it was called the Dragon-Tail Way. The main hall and the two pavilions, standing on the high brick terrace, combined with the stretching Dragon-Tail Way to create a vigorous architectural style in a period of great prosperity for the feudal society of China.

The remains of the Daming Palace, including bricks, roofing tiles, engraved paving tiles, stone column bases carved with lotus motif, glazed tiles, stone dragon-head gargoyles for leading rainwater away, stone posts, ridge ends with bird-tail or animal head motifs, etc., show clearly that the palaces of the Tang Dynasty were built on a huge scale. In the palaces there were many gigantic halls and magnificent buildings, as well as well-ornamented pavilions and covered walks connected to one another. It is really the same as described in the Tang poetry, or illustrated in the Tang murals, especially in the murals in Dunhuang Grottoes.

## V. Bianliang

Bianliang had been the capital of the Later Zhou, and was the capital of a prefecture called Bianzhou in the Tang Dynasty. The palatial city of the Song Court was then built and extended on the basis of the governmental building complex of the late satrap of the Tang Court. Zhao Kuangyin, later known as Emperor Taizu of the Song, issued an order to make drawings of the Tang palaces in Luoyang, and then built a replica in Bianliang. Palaces were grouped together in a walled enclosure called "Da Nei", namely, the Palatial City. Its perimeter is only five li in length, less than half of that of the Tang Palatial City in Chang'an. Its total area is less than that of the Daming Palace of the Tang Dynasty.

The palatial city was in the centre of Bianliang. Each side had a gate and each corner, a watchtower. The Gate of Red Phoenix was located in the centre of the southern wall, with five gate openings and a U-shaped plan. On a north-south street called Heavenly Street, a bridge called Zhou Qiao (Prefecture Bridge) was laid across the Bianhe River. To the south of the bridge, the governmental or administrative offices were located on the east and west sides of Heavenly Street. Outside the palatial city, there were still two layers of city walls. Each layer had a moat. Such a layout for three layers of walled enclosures, one inside another, was followed by the later dynasties of the Jin (Jurchen), Yuan (Mongol), Ming and Qing (Manchu). The main hall of the outer court in the palatial city was named the Hall of Great Rejoicing. To its north was the front hall called the Hall of Purple Polaris, which was one of the halls for the emperors to attend court and hold an audience. Besides, there were many other buildings in the outer court, such as the Hall of Governing by Noninterference, the Hall of Ease and Comfort, etc. Behind the outer court were the palaces and gardens of the inner court.

Since the Yellow River often overflowed its banks and caused serious flooding, Bianliang has been submerged in mud and silt layer by layer to a depth of more than 8 m. After a series of excavations, however, the features of the old capital have been revealed. But as no actual palatial buildings remain, we can only have a limited idea of their appearance from some ancient books and paintings, e.g., the paintings *Emperor Ming Going to the Summer Resort, Picture of the Han Palace, Boat Regatta in Brilliant Golden Pool*, and so on. From these, it seems the palace architecture in the Song Dynasty generally adopted the shape like the Chinese character "工", or with complicated roofs and eaves. Sometimes, a hall was built with a gable-and-hipped roof, sometimes with a cross-ridged roof with a gable at each of the four sides. Halls and palaces were richly decorated with wood members carved and painted, winding balustrades, making the structures like marble towers and jade houses. In short, in the Song Dynasty, palaces became more magnificent and more splendid.

## VI. Five Capitals

During the Northern and Southern Song periods, there arose the Liao (Khitan) and the Jin (Jurchen) dynasties one after the other in North and Northeast China. The Liao Dynasty had five capitals, the Upper, the Central, the Western, the Eastern and the Southern. Linhuang Prefecture was its Upper Capital, its site to the northeast of present-day Lindong County, Inner Mongolia. In the Upper Capital, there still exists a 500 $m^2$ terrace on which the palatial halls

**Remains of the Meridian Gate of the Ming Central Capital**

When the Ming Dynasty was founded in Nanjing, Zhu Yuanzhang, known as Emperot Taizu, built another imperial palace in his Central Capital Linhao (now Fengyang in Anhui Province). The palace there has long been demolished, but some remains still exist.

**Inner Golden River in the Early Ming Imperial Palace in Nanjing**

The Ming Dynasty was founded in 1368 with Nanjing as its capital. In 1375, the Imperial Palace was reconstructed. Since Zhu Di (Emperor Yongle) seized the throne, and the capital moved to Beijing, the Imperial Palace in Nanjing was neglected and eventually destroyed. Though it was restored, to a certain extent, under the reign of later emperors, it never resumed its original appearance.

used to be erected. The Southern Capital was named Xijin Prefecture, which is now Beijing. This capital was built up on the site of Youzhou of the Tang period. The Southern Capital was more magnificent.

The Jin Dynasty also had five capitals. Its Upper Capital, called Huining Prefecture, was located south of what is now Acheng County, Heilongjiang Province. There, the site of its palatial halls has been reduced to a square terrace, each side around 500 m. A historical record says, "the Upper Capital was an imitation of Bianliang, but its scale was only two to three-tenths that of the Song capital". Later, King Hailing of the Jin made Yanjing (now Beijing) the Central Capital.

The design of the city was carried out in the traditional ways of the Han.

Inside the imperial city, there were three palatial complexes as well as the imperial lake and the imperial garden. The palatial city, was the main complex, located on the southern end of the central axis. The imperial lake was situated to the west. On its west bank was the residence of the empress dowager which was the Palace of Prosperity and Happiness. To its north was the Palace of Prosperity and Holiness, where the princes resided. The imperial garden was situated on the north side. Outside the front entrance of the imperial city, which was known as the Gate of Succeeding to Heaven, there was a stone bridge and a pailou-like gateway Lingxing Men. In front of the Lingxing Men, the imperial road was placed running south to the front entrance of the capital city, which was named the Gate of Positive Elegance. On either side of the imperial road, the extremely long "Thousand-step Corridors" were located. Such a layout of the area in front of the imperial city of Dadu was similar to that of the Song

Bianliang and the Jin Central Capital. In Dadu, the imperial ancestral temple and the altar of land and grain had been built up to the east and to the west of the imperial city respectively, which followed the principles stipulated by the *Survey on Construction Work*.

Palaces of the Yuan period were much more splendid. Marco Polo, an Italian traveler, in his the *Travels of Marco Polo* writes, "The walls inside are covered with silver and gold and there are paintings of horsemen, dragons and every kind of bird and animal. The main reception room can seat more than 6,000 people. There is an overwhelming number of rooms; no architect in the world could have designed the palace better. The roof is beautifully painted in many colours—vermilion, green, blue, yellow and so forth—so that it shines like a jewel and can be seen from afar."

When the Ming Dynasty was founded, Zhu Yuanzhang, the first emperor, made Nanjing its capital. He built his palace in Nanjing first, and then started work on another in the Central Capital (now in Fengyang County, Anhui Province). However, the construction work of the latter was soon stopped as it would have been exhausting for the people and drained the treasury. Later on, the two palaces became the blueprints of the Forbidden City in Beijing.

# The Forbidden City in Beijing

## —— A Bright Pearl as a Crystallization of Wisdom and Hard Toil

The Forbidden City, or the Imperial Palace, in Beijing is the most magnificent among the existent palaces of the Qing Court. Though first laid out and established in the Ming Dynasty, many more halls and building complexes now existing were built up in the Qing Dynasty. Its large scale, and the huge area it covers, are matchless.

## I. Basis for Planning of the Forbidden City

Three imperial palaces were successively built in the early Ming Dynasty. The imperial palace in Beijing, known as the Forbidden City, was the third, erected under the imperial edict of Emperor Zhudi (whose reign title was Yongle). It is the sole imperial palace preserved intact in China. It carried on a fine tradition incorporating the experiences of past dynasties and brought forth many new ideas in the field of Chinese palace architecture. The Forbidden City is considered to synthesize and bring to the highest development all the architectural measures of previous dynasties.

### 1. Emperor - the Most Respected; Palace - the Capital Centre

In ancient China, it was a prevalent belief that the centre should be the most important and respected place. It was not unusual to choose a site for the capital in the centre of the country and to place the imperial palace in the centre of the capital. As Xun Zi, a scholar of the Warring States Periods, writes,"It is a rule of etiquette for the king to live in the centre of the country he dominates". The imperial palace was usually located on the north-south axis of the capital as to show the most respected position of the emperor. In the Ming Dynasty, the capital city of Beijing was built up on the basis of Dadu. Only some slight changes were made: the northern city wall being moved southward about 2,500 m and the southern city wall, southward about 500 m. The palatial city, i.e. the Forbidden City and the imperial city were laid out a little south of the central part of the capital. In the period of Ming Emperor Jiajing

**Panoramic View of the Three Great Halls**

Concepts underlying the design of the Forbidden City in Beijing embody supreme imperial power. The general planning and architectural arrangement highlight the feudal patriarchal clan system and symbolize the spirit of the imperial authority, a fact which is more important than practical functions. Major buildings are symmetrically arranged along a central axis to display regularity and dignity, with the Three Great Halls serving as the core of the complex. The Hall of Supreme Harmony, the venue for grand ceremonies, is the most significant building.

(1522~1565), another city wall was built and added to the southern side. The extended part of the capital was then called the Outer City, and the original part, the Inner City. The extension placed the Forbidden City right in the centre of the capital. Thereafter, the axial line of the Forbidden City extends southward to the Gate of Everlasting Stability, the southern central gate of the Outer City, and northward to the Bell and Drum Towers. The total length of the axial line is about 8,000 m, while the total length of the capital from north to south is 8,450 m. To the left (east) of the axial line, there is the Imperial Ancestral Temple, and to its right (west), the Altar of Land and Grain. In front of the imperial city, there was the Imperial Way just on the axial line, with government offices east and west of it. Inside of the Gate of Everlasting Stability, the Temple of Heaven was in the east, and the Altar of Agriculture, in the west. The arrangement of the imperial altars, temples and government offices on either side of the axial line in front of the Forbidden City was not only readily available for the emperor to held court, to offer sacrifices and to conduct state affairs, it also made the capital centre where the emperor resided and worked as prominent as possible. To the north of the imperial city, there was a market

forming the capital's shopping centre.

Beijing, capital of the Ming Dynasty, remains a living example of the layout of a capital, so as to place the palace in the centre, to make the Imperial Ancestral Temple and Altar of Land and Grain in front of the palace on the left and right, and the market in its rear. Such a capital city planning was worked out according to what *the Survey on Construction Work* indicated that the Zhou capital should comply with two thousand years ago: namely, an axial line passing through nearly the whole capital city from north to south, in the centre of which the palatial city is situated. Beijing, the capital of the Ming Dynasty, was not only incomparable with the Zhou capital, but also much more magnificent than Bianliang, capital of the Northern Song Dynasty.

**2. Five Gates and Three Courts; the Emperor in the Innermost**

*Mian*, an old poem collected in *the Book of Songs (Shi Jing)*, vividly depicts the process of Gugong Danfu's founding of the early Zhou capital and building his palace at Zhouyuan. It says, "So created is the front gate Gao Men of the capital city, which seems imposingly elevated; and then, erected is the front gate Ying Men of the palatial city, which appears dazzlingly upraised." The gates stood tall and broad. Why did they make their entrance gates so gigantic as described in the verses?

As a rule, the place where the emperor lived and worked had to be enclosed

**Full View of the Gate of Supreme Harmony**

The Gate of Supreme Harmony was originally built in 1420, or the 18th year of the reign of Ming Emperor Yongle. The existing structure was rebuilt in 1889, or the 15th year in the reign of Qing Emperor Guangxu. The Gate of Supreme Harmony is flanked by two smaller gates – the Gate of Luminous Virtue to the east and the Gate of Correct Conduct to the west. The Inner Golden River flows through the courtyard in front of the Gate from culverts beneath the western suite of galleries to the eastern suite. Five white marble bridges span the river, with the centre bridge on the central axis set aside for the exclusive use of the emperor.

by layers of walls with their entrance gates closely guarded. There were many scholars devoted to researches on palatial gates all through the ages. Zhu Xi, a scholar in the Song Dynasty, relates that in the time of Gugong Danfu, there were no rules and regulations for erecting gates, therefore he only built two for himself. Later on, when the Zhou Court seized power, the two gates, Gao Men and Ying Men, were then assigned as the specific gates for the King of the Zhou Court. Dukes and princes were not allowed to build such two gates.

Synthesizing the opinions of various schools, we find that according to the ritual system of the Zhou, there were five gates for the king: Gao Men, Ku Men, Zhi Men, Ying Men and Lu Men successively. Gao Men was the farthest gate; Ku Men was a gate for storage; Zhi Men was a gate like today's Meridian Gate with a U-shaped plan; Ying Men was the gate for the king passing through to conduct the state affairs; and Lu Men was the entrance to the king's residence. If one was allowed to meet the king, one had to pass through these five gates.

Zheng Xuan, a scholar of the Han Dynasty, in his *Commentary to the Book of Rites* pointed out that an emperor should have nine gates: Besides the five aforementioned, there were still the City Gate, Gate of Suburbs, Gate of Outer Suburbs, and the Pass Gate.

In the old ages, gates were closely related to Courts. According to *the Ritual of Zhou*, there used to be three Courts in the Zhou Dynasty, i.e., one Outer Court and two Inner Courts. The inner courts were again divided into a Zhi

Court and a Yan Court.

The Qin Dynasty adopted a new system of prefectures and counties to replace the old system of feudal feoffs, and established a centralized government under the reign of the autocratic emperor.

In the later dynasties, to hold grand ceremonies, to hold courts and to grant titles could not be the same as that under the Zhou. The names of the Courts were also different from those of the Zhou. The Courts were usually divided into Daily Court, Constant Court, Morning Court and Midday Court, etc. They also had relevant halls, such as the Main Hall, the Front Hall, the Hall for Banquet, the Ordinary Hall, etc. However, the system of Gates and Courts laid out from south to north was still unchanged. It also greatly influenced the layout of palace buildings.

The following is the layout of the buildings on the axial line of the Forbidden City. It shows that a system of Gates and Courts similar to the Zhou Dynasty, but their names and amounts differ.

The Gate of Great Qing (or the Gate of Great Ming in the Ming Dynasty,

**The Meridian Gate**

The Meridian Gate was originally built in 1420, or the 18th year in the reign of Ming Emperor Yongle. The existing gate and auxiliary buildings on the platform were rebuilt in 1647, or the 4th year in the reign of Qing Emperor Shunzhi. Ming and Qing emperors used the gate as a venue for presenting prisoners of war.

or the Gate of China since the revolution of 1911) is usually referred to as the southernmost entrance to the Forbidden City. To name the gate after the name of the country might imply that the gate is the entrance to the country. Inside the Gate of Great Qing, there was a long narrow courtyard. Its function was somewhat like that of the Outer Court in the Zhou Dynasty. As the society developed, things like consultation with common people no longer existed, while the grand ceremonies were held in the Three Great Halls.

Inside the Gate of Great Qing to the north end of the courtyard is the Gate of Heavenly Peace (Tian An Men), the front gate of the Imperial City, which was called the Gate of Receiving Mandate of Heaven (Cheng Tian Men) in the Ming Dynasty. It is a massive building with a magnificent gate tower used as a rostrum built on the projected platform of the city wall. It was about the same as Gao Men of the Zhou Dynasty.

Inside the Gate of Heavenly Peace is the Gate of Correct Demeanor (Duan Men). According to the explanation of the Five Gates by the Song scholar Zhu Xi, this might be the Ku Men. However, there are no records that anything was stored in the Gate of Correct Demeanor in the Ming-Qing periods. To its east and west, there are really two gates to the Imperial Ancestral Temple and the Altar of Land and Grain respectively.

To the north of the Gate of Correct Demeanor is the Meridian Gate, the front entrance to the Forbidden City. The Meridian Gate has two frontal wings forming a U-shaped plan. The wings are referred to as Double Guan or Double Que. The U-plan gate is just the form of Zhi Men of the Zhou Dynasty.

Inside the Meridian Gate, there is the Gate of Supreme Harmony (originally called the Gate for Paying Tribute to Heaven and later renamed as the Gate of Imperial Supremacy in the Ming Period). According to a rule formulated in the early Ming Dynasty, it was the place where the Ming emperors to practice "governing the state from the imperial gate", conducting state affairs there every morning. Officials and officers came to the courtyard in front of the gate and stood there in prescribed order. The emperor sat on a throne temporarily moved onto the terrace. He heard reports or memorials from below, handled court affairs and made decisions. Hence the Gate of Supreme Harmony might correspond to Ying Men of the Zhou Dynasty.

Passing through the Gate of Supreme Harmony, one comes to a courtyard where the three great halls stand on a three-tiered terrace: Hall of Supreme Harmony, Hall of Complete Harmony and Hall of Preserving Harmony. Here, the emperor held grand ceremonies, accepted congratulations and entertained distinguished guests, etc. The courtyard is large enough to hold hundreds of officials, officers and honor guards. In the Zhou Dynasty, such activities were carried out in the ancestral temple or the king's living quarter, while in the Ming-Qing periods, a splendid palatial building complex was specially built.

The Gate of Heavenly Purity, corresponding to the Lu Men of the Zhou Court, is on the dividing line between the outer and inner courts.

Inside the Gate of Heavenly Purity is the Palace of Heavenly Purity, the main hall in the emperor's living quarter also used for him to hear memorials, give audiences to higher officials, as well offering entertainment on festivals such as the Lunar New Year's Day, Mid-autumn Festival, Winter Solstice, the Emperor's Birthday. It had the same function as the Yan Court in the Zhou Dynasty.

To the south of the Gate of Great Qing, there are three other gates on the city's axial line, two on the inner city wall (i.e. the South-Facing Gate and the

**The Gate of Heavenly Purity**

A view of the Gate of Heavenly Purity from the three-tiered terrace in the outer court. Attendant houses, which sit outside the gate on the left and right, were built to provide shelter for Qing princes, dukes, ministers and higher officials awaiting an imperial audience. The gate opens to the residences and living quarters of the empress and imperial concubines. The arrangement conforms to the following Zhou Dynasty rule for Lu Men (Lu Gate):"Nine houses for female attendants should be inside the gate, and nine houses for the ministers awaiting for imperial audiences should be outside the gate".

gate under the Arrow Tower), and the third forming the front entrance to the Outer City (i.e. the Gate of Everlasting Stability). In addition to the six gates mentioned above, in front of the emperor's living quarter, there are nine gates in total. All face south.

### 3. Outer Court and Inner Court; Six Palaces and Six Living Quarters

The Forbidden City was divided into two halves, the southern half being for the emperor to hold grand ceremonies and to hear officials' memorials, and the northern half being the imperial family's living quarters. The Gate of Heavenly Purity is on the dividing line. In the Qing Dynasty, the southern half was called the "outer court" and the northern half, the "inner court".

Division of a palace into outer and inner parts had been a traditional measure all along.

As the outer court was a symbol of imperial power, two main parts had to be placed in it. They were the courtyard for holding court and the halls for

**The Palace of Heavenly Purity**

The Plalace of Heavenly Purity was originally built in 1421, or the 19th year in the reign of Ming Emperor Yongle. The palace was restored and renovated on several occasions, and the existing structure was rebuilt in 1797, or the 2nd year in the reign of Qing Emperor Jiaqing. The elevated walkway in front of the palace leading to the Gate of Heavenly Purity enabled passing through the gate to reach the palace without climbing stairways. The rather small courtyard in front of the palace offers a cordial and harmonious environment.

**The Hall of Imperial Peace**

The Hall of Imperial Peace, located north of the Imperial Garden, was built in 1535, or the 14th year in the reign of Ming Emperor Jiajing. The Lod of Black, or God of Water was enshrined in the Hall.

performing ceremonies. In the outer court of the Forbidden City, on the east and west sides of the three great halls, are the side suites of rooms, mostly used as storehouses for articles of tribute, such as various kinds of delicious food, suits of armor, saddles and bridles, silks and satins, porcelain, copper ware, etc. To the east of the courtyard, was the imperial stable. According to the ritual system, "When the ruler establishes his palaces and houses, he should build first the ancestral temple, then the stable and storehouse, and, at last, the halls and residences". This was to show that the ruler would worship his ancestors and would live a prosperous and peaceful life. Such an arrangement is based on *the book of Rites* (Li Ji).

In the inner court of the Forbidden City, were mainly the residential buildings and gardens for the imperial family.

In the earliest ages, there really had been some rules about the layout of the palaces. In *the Ritual of Zhou*, "six palaces" and "six living quarters" are mentioned. According to the records, the emperor attended court every morning, then came back to the major living quarter (Lu Qin) to give an audience, and then to a minor living quarter (Yan Qin) to change his clothes. It was recorded that the emperor had six living quarters, one major and five minor. The major quarter was used for the emperor to accept officials and to conduct state affairs; the minor quarters were the places for the emperor to live in or rest with the imperial concubines in attendance. The empress also had six living quarters, called "six palaces", again one major and five minor. The major palace also had the function of conducting affairs.

The layout of the inner court of the Forbidden City is similar to the arrangement as mentioned above.

**4. Yin, Yang and Five Elements; Palaces to Symbolize Constellations**

"Yin" and "yang" primarily denote forward towards and backward from the sun, respectively. *The Book of Changes* writes, "Yin combined with yang is called the doctrine". The combination of yin and yang is regarded as the law of changes of all things in the world. Everything has the two aspects of yin and yang. They are mutually opposing and dependent on each other for existence. For example, the direction or position is above and below, front and back, or left and right; numbers are odds and evens.

The term 'five elements', or Wu Xing, first appeared in *the Book of History* (Shu Jing). They are wood, fire, earth, metal and water which represent the five different kinds of matter that people constantly come in contact with. Later on, the theory of five elements was combined with the principles of yin and yang, as well as those of the geomantic omen and the interaction between nature and human beings. It made the implication of five elements developed and expanded. Therefore, many other fields were connected with and related to the five elements. For example, the five colours are: green (or blue), red, yellow, white and black; the five directions: east, south, centre, west and north; the five stages of life: birth, growth, synthesis, gathering and hiding; the five musical notes: jue, zhi, gong, shang and yu; etc. Even the four seasons, spring, summer, autumn and winter, are also related to the five elements. An extension of the theory is the mutual production and the mutual destruction between two of the five elements. The mutual production is that wood produces fire, fire produces earth, earth produces metal, metal produces water and water produces wood. The mutual destruction is that wood destroys earth, earth destroys water, water destroys fire, fire destroys metal and metal destroys wood. These theories prevailed throughout ancient times in China, and were considered as unchangeable truth, and the law of interaction of all things in the material universe. It was believed that the relationship between the five elements had to be straightened out, otherwise disasters or inauspicious developments might occur. Such thoughts made things more and more mysterious. Architecture has

**Roofs of the Three Rear Palaces**

Emperor Wudi of the Western Han Dynasty based his dynasty on the morality of the earth, as the earth corresponded to the yellow colour according to the five-element theory. Therefore, yellow became a symbol of the imperial power of the Han Court, and yellow was considered as an esteemed colour during the Yuan, Ming and Qing dynasties. Hence, nearly all roofs in the Forbidden City were covered with yellow glazed tiles. Yellow symbolized the earth, and the earth symbolized the country.

been an important social activity, so it could not but follow the principles and theories of this kind.

As for the general layout of the palaces, the palatial halls were all oriented and situated in the light of these theories. The south symbolizes growth and corresponds to fire. It is best suited for holding court, therefore the Outer Court was situated in the south. The north symbolizes hiding and corresponds to water. It is best suited for living and resting, therefore the Inner Court was situated in the north. The buildings and building complexes for civil administration, such as the Grand Secretariat, the Pavilion of Literary Profundity, the Hall of Literary Glory, etc., were all located in the east, for the east symbolized the spring and corresponded to wood. Those for defense preparations, such as the Hall of Military Eminence, the Military Pavilion, etc., were all located in the west, for the west symbolized autumn and corresponded to metal. The Grand Council was the former Military Council. Its office was located on the west wing outside the Gate of Heavenly Purity.

The life stage of the empress dowager and imperial concubine dowagers stood for gathering with the direction in the west, corresponding to metal of the five elements. Since the Han Dynasty, the empress dowagers' palaces, or residences were usually located in the west. Hence in the Ming and Qing dynasties, the Hall of Compassion and Tranquility, the Hall of Tranquil Old Age and the Hall of Longevity and Good Health were all located in the west of the Forbidden City. The life stage of the young princes stood for growth with the direction in the east, corresponding to wood. Therefore, the prince's palace was called the "Eastern Palace" in ancient times. The Hall of Literary Glory in the Forbidden City used to be the Eastern Palace in the early Ming Period. During the period of the Qing Emperor Qianlong, the three south lodges were built in the east of the Forbidden City for the princes to live and study in. The north stands for water. The traditional timber-framed structures were liable to be destroyed by fire, and the fire might be destroyed by water, so that the Lord of Black, or the God of Water, was enshrined in the Hall of Imperial Peace, the main building in the imperial garden located on the northernmost end of the axial line. The front entrance of the imperial garden was called "the Gate of Heaven the First", the name of which was given from the old saying "Heaven the first begets water". The Hall of Imperial Peace was built on a Sumeru terrace with marble balustrades. The balustrade at the centre of the northern side was carved in a motif of sea waves. It also implied the auspicious meaning that water might destroy fires.

Located in the south, the outer court stands for yang, where the palatial halls were laid out more openly and sparsely. There, the buildings were designed to be magnificent and imposing to meet the needs of holding court. All these measures brought about an atmosphere of manly hardiness. On the central axis, there is the complex of the three great halls, and on the lateral axis, there is the complex of the Palace of Literary Glory on the left (east), and that of the Palace of Military Eminence on the right (west). The palatial complexes also totalled the odd number "three" which implies the sun, the moon and the stars as well as the so-called "three enclosures" of the constellations. Bridges across the Inner Golden River, steps up to the terrace, and layers of brickwork of either the terrace or the wall beneath windows are all in odd numbers, representing yang.

Located in the north, the inner court stands for yin, where the palaces are compactly laid out, the building sizes are relatively smaller than those in the outer court, and both the exterior and interiors are more ornamental and offer richer flavors of life. All these measures demonstrate an atmosphere of womanly softness. During the early Ming period, only two buildings were erected on the axial line, i.e. the Palace of Heavenly Purity and that of Earthly Tranquility. On the left and right sides, each had six palaces. This is why the total number of lodges which is even was made from two odd numbers. In the Inner Court, the layers of brick wall dadoes and the steps up to the terraces are all in even numbers.

The changes of yin and yang integrated with the ancient rites long guided imperial palace design.

In the five-element theory, colours correspond to directions, i.e. green (or blue) stands for the east, red for the south, white for the west, black for the

**Panoramic View of the Gate of Tranquil Longevity and the Hall of Imperial Supremacy**

The Gate of Tranquil Longevity, built in 1772, or the 37th year in reign of Emperor Qianlong, is located north of the Gate of Imperial Supremacy. The Gate of Tranquil Longevity is flanked by two slanting screen walls fronted by a pair of gilded bronze lions. The Hall of Imperial Supremacy is the front hall in the palatial complex of the Palace of Tranquil Longevity. The Hall is similar to the Palace of Heavenly Purity in style and form, and is of the slightly lower rank than the Hall of Supreme Harmony in style and form. A 1.6 m high elevated pathway in front of the Hall of Imperial Supremacy leads to the Gate of Tranquil Longevity.

north, dark for the heaven and yellow for the earth. It was said that the Zhou Court was based on the morale of fire, so that the Zhou people revered red colour, and the columns of the palatial halls were all painted red. Emperor Wudi of the Han Dynasty confirmed his dynasty to be based on the morale of earth, therefore yellow became a symbol of royal power. Yellow was also esteemed in the Yuan, Ming and Qing dynasties. This is the reason why an overwhelming majority of the building roofs in the Forbidden City are covered with yellow glazed tiles. Yellow symbolizes the earth which is located in the middle or the centre and represents the whole nation. As in the five-element theory, the earth is produced by fire, and fire stands for the red colour, so that the columns, doors and windows in palatial buildings are usually painted red to signify the prosperity and vitality of the country. The three south lodges used as the residences of the young princes were erected in the years of Emperor Qianlong in the Qing Dynasty. Their roofs are all covered with green glazed tiles, for these buildings are situated in the east of the Forbidden City, and the east symbolizes wood of the five elements, whose colour is green. In ancient times, the princes' palace was usually named "the Green Palace". Inside the north gate, the Gate of Divine Might, of the Forbidden City, there are two rows of buildings in the east and west. The roofs of these buildings are covered with black glazed tiles, for they are located in the northernmost of the city, and the north symbolizes water, whose colour is black.

The Forbidden City was laid out on a relatively smooth plain without mountains and waters. When it was first built, the waterways were dredged from the Yuquan Hill (Hill of Jade Spring) in the western suburbs. Water was channeled into the imperial city and the Forbidden City. As the water comes from the west, and the west stands for metal or gold, which produces water according to the five-element theory, it was named the inner or outer golden river according to its situation. The earth excavated from the moat around the Forbidden City and dug up from the Imperial Lake to the west of the moat was used to make a 52 m high hill, called Prospect Hill, to the north of the Forbidden City, making the palaces in a situation "with hills behind and water in front", which was based on the ancient geomantic feng-shui (wind and water) theory for the planning the capital. In order to exterminate the shades and forms of the previous dynasty, the Prospect Hill was built just on the site of the demolished palace of the Yuan Court.

### 5. Timber-Framed Structure; Composition of Courtyards

In traditional Chinese architecture, an individual building is composed of several "jian" or bays. A jian is referred to as the basic unit of a building. Several buildings laid out on a rectangular site constitute a courtyard. There are thousands of buildings enclosed in some 90 courtyards in the Forbidden City, which are arranged longitudinally to form a number of north-south axes, among which the central axis passing through the entire city is the main one. Moreover, the Gate of Supreme Harmony is regarded as the centre of the outer court. To its east is the palatial complex of the Hall of Literary Glory; and to its west is the Hall of Military Eminence. The gate and the two complexes are located on an east-west line, forming the lateral subsidiary axis of the outer court. In the Qing Dynasty, to the east of the Gate of Heavenly Purity, a palatial complex, with the Hall of Imperial Supremacy in its centre, was erected. This was used as the living quarters of the emperor's father who had abdicated. To the west of that gate, another palatial complex with the Hall of Compassion and Tranquility at its centre, was erected as the living quarters of the empress dowagers. Each palatial complex has a north-south axis. To the left and right of the Palace of Heavenly Purity, there are the east and west six palaces as well as the east and west five lodges, thus forming some other secondary north-south axes, which are set on the two sides of the central axis of the city. The layout of the axes may be clearly differentiated between what is primary and what is secondary.

All the major buildings in the Forbidden City are set on its south-north

**Side View of the Gate of Supreme Harmony**

The Gate of Supreme Harmony, built during the early Ming period, was originally known as the Gate for Paying Tribute to Heaven. The name was changed to the Gate of Imperial Supremacy during the reign of Ming Emperor Jiajing, with the present name adopted during the early Qing period. The Gate of Supreme Harmony is nine bays in length and has double-eaved gable-and-hipped roof. The gate sits on a white marble terrace, with beams and lintels decorated with hexi decorative paintings of gilded dragon patterns.

central axial line. The overall length of the axial line from the Gate of Great Qing in the south to the Prospect Hill in the north is about three odd km. Traditional Chinese artistic concepts applied to organizing the space according to functional requirements, and using the magnificence of architecture to deeply impress people with heartfelt fear and worship of imperial power.

Inside the Gate of Great Qing, there lies the imperial way running straight to the north, 60 m wide and 550 m long. In front of the Tian An Men Gate (Gate of Heavenly Peace), the imperial way is widened to 350 m to make the gate visually pleasing. Inside the Gate of Heavenly Peace, there is an enlarged enclosed courtyard 110 m wide and approximately square. Inside the Gate of Correct Demeanor is another enlarged courtyard with the same width, but its north-south length is three times longer. The Meridian Gate stands at the northern end of this courtyard. Inside the Meridian Gate, there is a 200 m wide courtyard in front of the Gate of Supreme Harmony. Passing through it, there appears the largest courtyard with the three great halls in the centre. This courtyard has the same width and a north-south length twice that of the courtyard outside the Gate of Supreme Harmony. A series of enlarged courtyards are laid out from south to north in such a way that the mighty atmosphere of imperial power grows steadily to a climax with the three great halls.

Thereafter, the architectural scale becomes progressively reduced. Either the width or the length of the main courtyard in the inner court, where the three rear palaces are located on the central axial line, is only a half of that of the main courtyard in the outer court, though the layouts of the halls in the two courtyards are similar in form and style.

Along with the enlargement of the courtyards in the outer court, the buildings vary correspondingly in size, exterior and interior, as well as furnishings to create various environmental atmosphere.

The Gate of Great Qing was an entrance building with only three bays. Inside it, the thousand-step-corridors on either side of the imperial way were built in equal bays with quite thrifty and simple facades, forming a trend toward the palaces ahead.

The Gate of Heavenly Peace has a magnificent gate tower built on a high projected platform of the city wall. The gate tower is nine bays in length (east-west), five bays in depth (south-north) and 33.7 m in height. The number nine combined with the number five embodies the most revered and respected. It means that building of this kind could only be erected in the imperial palace

**Section of a Gilded Bronze Vat in Front of the Hall of Supreme Harmony**

Iron and bronze water vats sit at the sides of major buildings in the Forbidden City. The external surfaces of most important vats are gilded and have a pair of loop handles.

**Bronze Tripod in Front of the Hall of Supreme Harmony**

Tripods in the Forbidden City not only symbolize the high prestige and outstanding achievements of the emperor, but also served a functional purpose as incense burners. Smoke from burning incense creates a cloudy and misty atmosphere which added respect and dignity to grand ceremonies held in the Hall of Supreme Harmony.

and used for the emperors. In front of the gate, there is the outer golden river flowing from the west to the east. Five arched marble bridges are placed across the river. This imitates the Magpie Bridge across the Silver River (the Milky Way) in Heaven. Either inside or outside of the gate, there are two ornamental stone columns to indicate that it is the front entrance to the Forbidden City. The white marble balustrades standing crisscross along the river banks and bridges, the stone-carved columns towering aloft, all the surroundings set off the red-walled and yellow-tile-roofed Gate of Heavenly Peace, create a resplendent and magnificent atmosphere peculiar to the imperial court.

The Gate of Correct Demeanor is the same as the Gate of Heavenly Peace in form and size including the height. Traveling northward from the Gate of Great Qing along the central axis, one may find the buildings gradually become taller and taller, but the Gate of Correct Demeanor is an exception. As a repetition of its former building, it foreshadows what is to follow in size and height.

The Meridian Gate is the front entrance to the Forbidden City. Since the ancient times, a gate of this kind, usually called "Que", has long been peculiar to the imperial palace as its main entrance. The Meridian Gate is the tallest building in the Forbidden City with a total height of 37.95 m. Being the main entrance, not only is it magnificent, it is also used as a defense works. Standing in front, facing the three-sided red walls with tall and erect watchtowers on the tops, one feels oppressed by the chilly, stern and solemn atmosphere.

The Gate of Supreme Harmony is only 23.8 m high, much lower than the Meridian Gate, for it is not a city gate, and it can only be erected on a rather low terrace. No longer to show the reverence and respect by building mass and height, the gate is strengthened by the composition of its surroundings. In front

**Bird's Eye View of a Corner Watchtower**

Watchtowers standing at all four corners of the city wall are turret-style structures with triple-eaved cross-ridged roofs. The upper section of the roofs are formed by two perpendicular horizontal ridges with four gablets facing outward and a pommel at the centre of the intersection point. Double-eaved gable-and-hipped roofs are attached to four sides of the two lower levels. The complicated roof structures of the watchtowers constitute an ingenious combination of 72 horizontal and sloping ridges on triple-eaved roofs.

of the gate, a pair of bronze lions standing on either side, the inner golden river snakes its way west to east, across the enlarged courtyard, forming a tranquil and dignified environment.

The three great halls are situated on a three-tiered terrace in the centre of the enlarged courtyard inside the Gate of Supreme Harmony. The Hall of Supreme Harmony is the main one, so it is located on the highest level of the central axial line. In front, there are a number of stone and bronze sculptures to symbolize the impregnability and longevity of the imperial power. A stone sundial, a pavilion-shaped stone stand with a bronze standard measure housed in, a bronze tortoise and a bronze crane are placed on the terrace. Both the tortoise and the crane are incense burners. The incense is burned in their abdominal cavities and smoke curling up from their mouths. Nearby are several rows of bronze tripods for burning incense placed on either side of the flights of steps up to the terrace. When a grand ceremony was held, the smoke of burning incense would make the surroundings cloudy and misty. Lying prone on the steps to the terrace as an official had to do, and looking into the Hall at a distance, one would find that the Hall of Supreme Harmony indistinct in the clouds of smoke. In addition, the glittering yellow glazed tile roofing set off the blue sky. How could the civil officials and the military officers not but be provoked to worship the emperor in such circumstances?

According to a conception of the ritual system in ancient China, the greater, the taller and the more decorative a building, the more dignified it is. As *the Book of Rites* (Li Ji) states,"Rites, some are dignified for their quantity, some for their mass, some for their heights and some for their decorations". The Hall of Supreme Harmony has the largest number of bays, the largest floor area and the most splendid decoration, so that it is the most dignified of all buildings in the Forbidden City. Only the Meridian Gate is an exception for its special form and style. The other buildings are all of lower positions, in some respects, such as mass, size, height, roof style, decorative painting standard, projection of bracket sets, etc. This is the reason why the buildings are of similar exteriors, but different in details.

## II. Architectural Design

The huge palatial building complexes of the Forbidden City not only embodied the imperial power, they were also places in which the emperor

Corner Watchtower and Moat

The moat surrounding the Forbidden City was the first line of defense for the imperial palace. The wide moat and high brick city wall with watchtowers at the four corners and four entrance gates formed an impregnable system of defense.

and the imperial family worked and lived. In order to demonstrate imperial dignity and the impregnability of imperial power, the design of the complexes accentuated the facilities and installations for the emperor and his family to hold courts, to live in, enjoy some recreation and to offer sacrifices. Many measures were also adopted in the architectural design to fit in with the changes of the weather, especially with those of the four seasons.

### 1. The City Walls and the Moat

In ancient times, the palatial city was also called the forbidden inner. It was a restricted zone, closely guarded to ensure the emperor's absolute safety. The walled enclosure of the Forbidden City was built thick and high, and the moat was wide and deep, forming a strongly fortified position.

The moat around the Forbidden City is 52 m wide and 6 m deep. Its revetments are built vertically with range stone walls, and the moat bed is paved with rectangular stone slabs. It is hard to negotiate the moat, even when it dries up.

**Imperial Throne in the Hall of Supreme Harmony**

The imperial throne, which is surrounded by six gilded coiled-dragon columns in the rear part of the central bay of the Hall of Supreme Harmony, sits on a dais with flights of seven steps to the front and on either side. A large seven panel screen sits behind the throne.

The walled enclosure is 9.9 m high with a thickness of 8.62 m at the base and 6.6 m at the top. A crenelated parapet is built along the outer side, while a plain parapet marks the inner side. All facing bricks were polished individually so that the wall surface appeared smooth and was hard to climb.

Each of the four sides of the walled enclosure has a gate. On the southern side is the Meridian Gate, the main entrance to the Forbidden City. It has a platform three m higher than the city wall. In the middle of the platform is a 9-bay-long and 5-bay-deep gate tower, which was a huge hall with a roof hipped and double-eaved, covered with yellow glazed tiles. A throne was placed in the hall. When the ceremony of presenting war prisoners was held after a triumphant expedition, the emperor would be present. A bell and a drum used to be placed on either side of the tower, to be struck while the ceremonies were being held or the emperor was passing through the gate. On both sides of the platform, there are two wings projecting southward, forming a U-shape, each with a 13-bay-long gallery, called "gallery of wild goose wing". On each end of the gallery is a turret-like square pavilion. A three-sided square with five lofty towers connected by galleries formed the specific feature of the Meridian Gate, known as "the five phoenix towers".

Watchtowers identical in form and style were erected on each of the four corners of the city wall. But due to their exquisite appearance and ingenious construction, the watchtowers became more decorative to the Forbidden City. The towers are 27.5 m high from ground level. Each has a square plan in the centre with three bays and a length of 8.73 m on each side. Attached to each central bay of the four sides is a veranda without exposed columns. The eight gable-and-hipped (xieshan) roofs formed three layers of eaves. Each gable-and-hipped roof has nine sloping and horizontal ridges, so that the ridges of a corner watchtower totalled seventy-two. A story about the construction of the corner watchtowers recounts that the designer wanted to work out an ideal design. Even though he forgot to eat and sleep while working, still he could not work it out. Master Lu Ban, the founder of the craft of carpenters was deeply touched by this and descended from Heaven. When the master appeared with a grasshopper cage in his hand, the designer suddenly saw the light. At last, a splendid watchtower was built up. Although a fairy tale, it reflects the fact that people had mysterious feelings about the watchtower.

### 2. Halls in the Outer Court

In the centre of the outer court are the three great halls or the three great audience halls, i.e. the Halls of Supreme Harmony, Complete Harmony and Preserving Harmony (originally named as the Halls of Serving Heaven, Splendid Canopy and Respectful Care in the early Ming Period; later renamed as the Halls of Imperial Supremacy, Middle Supremacy and Establishing Supremacy).

**Hall of Supreme Harmony** The name of the Hall implies that things in the universe are all related to and harmonized with one another. It is not only the largest hall in the Forbidden City, but also the largest timber-framed structure with the highest ranking still existing in the entire country. Its total length is 60.01 m, and total depth, 33.33 m, constituting a platform area of 2,377 $m^2$. As a "jian" is defined as the space bounded by four timber columns, the Hall of Supreme Harmony totalled 55 jian. The major columns are 1.06 m in

**Pavilion of Literary Profundity**

The Pavilion of Literary Profundity sits to the east of the three great halls and north of the Hall of Literary Glory in the outer court. The existing building was built in 1774, or the 39th year in the reign of Emperor Qianlong. The structure's roof is covered with blacck glazed tiles on sloping surfaces edged with green glazed tiles. The horizontal ridge is decorated and carved with patterns of dragons and waves, and exposed columns are painted green. The colour scheme in the Pavilion of Literary Profundity forms a unique feature amongst the yellow roofs and red walls in the Forbidden City.

diametre. The total height of the hall from ground level to the top of the ridge-end finials (including the height of the three-tiered terrace) is 37.44 m. It is the highest building in the Forbidden City.

In the centre of the Hall of Supreme Harmony the imperial throne was placed, with a caisson ceiling above and four gilded-dragon columns. In front of the throne, were the furnishings symbolizing the stability of the empire and implying propitiousness. When an important ceremony was held, incense was burned and the imperial guards of honor were arranged in two rows, holding utensils, such as battle-axes, halberds, umbrellas, flags, etc., from the terrace apron in front of the hall, through the Gate of Supreme Harmony, the Meridian Gate and the Gate of Correct Demeanor, right to the Gate of Heavenly Peace. In the period of Emperor Kangxi, the honor guards totalled over 3000.

**Hall of Complete Harmony** Being square, and surrounded by verandas, this is a pavilion-shaped hall with three bays on each side and a single-eaved pyramidal roof. Its platform has sides 24.1 m long. It is located between the two larger halls, bringing about a visual effect as if the three great halls were connected with one another. The Hall of Complete Harmony was a place for the emperor to rest temporarily before holding a ceremony, hence an imperial throne was installed.

**Hall of Preserving Harmony** In the Ming Dynasty, when ceremonies such as the crowning of the empress or the bestowing of a princely title were to be held, this hall was the place where the emperor wore the crown and the imperial dress for receiving congratulations in the ceremonies. In the Qing Dynasty, the emperors usually made the Hall of Preserving Harmony as a banquet hall to entertain the princes, dukes and ministers, and later on, as the place where the imperial examinations were held. The hall is of nine bays, slightly inferior to the Hall of Supreme Harmony. Its platform is 49.68 m in length and 24.97 m in depth. An imperial throne was installed in its centre.

**Hall of Literary Glory** It is a building complex located to the east of the Gate of Supreme Harmony. The complex was first built in 1420 (18th year of the Yongle Period), but destroyed by fire in the last years of the Ming Dynasty. It was rebuilt in the original form and style in 1683 (the 22nd year of the reign of Emperor Kangxi) in the Qing Dynasty. Two main halls are located on a 1.5-metre-high platform with a plan like the Chinese character "工", the Hall of Literary Glory in front and the Hall of Holding Respect in the rear, with a terrace in the front and a corridor connecting the two halls. Both are painted with hexi decorative paintings in golden dragon patterns and both have a single-eaved gable-and-hipped roof covered with yellow glazed tiles. The Hall of Literary Glory is 5 bays in length totalling 30.5 m and 3 bays in depth with a three-jumped (single tier of qiao and double tiers of ang) bracket system.

The Hall of Holding Respect is similar to the front hall, but it has less depth with a double-jumped bracket system. Two side halls are situated in front of the main halls: the Hall of Benevolence on the left (east) and the Hall of Righteousness on the right (west). Each has 5 bays in length with bracket sets without "jumps". These halls are enclosed by red washed walls, forming a rectangular courtyard. On its southern side is the entrance to the courtyard, the Gate of Literary Glory. This is a typical layout of the palatial complex in the Forbidden City: two main halls, one behind the other, located on the central axis, with two side halls on either side, which are inferior to the main ones in mass and size.

**Pavilion of Literary Profundity** It is the largest library in the Forbidden City. In the Ming Period, the Pavilion of Literary Profundity was located in front of Hall of Literary Glory, and built for keeping the rare books printed during the Song and Yuan periods, as well as the Ming encyclopedia Yongle Da Dian. Destroyed by fire, the Pavilion of Literary Profundity was rebuilt under the reign of the Qing Emperor Qianlong in 1774, on the Ming ruins of the Hall of Ancient Physicians. The structure of the new library was modelled on the Pavilion of Heaven the First at Ningbo, Zhejiang Province. It has five-and-a-half bays 34.7 m long, and three bays with front and rear verandas totalling 17.4 m wide. It is two-storeyed in appearance, but three-storeyed in fact, due to the presence of a mezzanine between the two main storeys. It has a gable-and-hipped roof covered with black glazed tiles on its sloping surfaces edged with green glazed tiles. The main ridge is decorated with purple dragons and coloured tiles on a green background. The walls are built of polished bricks with thinner joints. Each of the two side walls has an opening surmounted by a canopy in the form of a lean-to roof decorated with green glazed tiles. The columns are painted dark green. Decorative paintings on lintels and beams are all in Suzhou-style with patterns of literature motifs. The paintings and ornaments are all unique to the Forbidden City. All these measures imply that there would be no fire and everything would go well.

**Hall of Military Eminence** The layout of this palatial building complex is similar to that of the Hall of Literary Glory. In the early Ming Period, emperors used to live here for abstinence and to occasionally summon the ministers. When the early Qing Emperor Shunzhi had not yet moved his throne to Beijing, Duoergun, prince regent of the early Qing Court, handled official business here. Li Zicheng, a peasant leader lived here when he proclaimed himself emperor. In the northwest of the complex, there is a three-bayed building called the Hall of Bathing in Moral Integrity. To its north, is a domed building, with the interior of the dome finished in white glazed facing bricks. There is a circular opening at the top of the dome for lighting and ventilation, and hot water pipes have been installed.

### 3. Palaces in the Inner Court

All the palaces in the inner court were enclosed by a high red wall with a perimeter of about 1,500 m. When the palaces were first built, there were only four gates to the inner court, named Heavenly Purity, Earthly Tranquility,

**Gilded Bronze Lions Fronting of the Gate of Heavenly Purity**

The seven pairs of lions in the Forbidden City were cast during the Ming and Qing dynasties. Each pair includes a male lion with its right paw resting on a ball to the left and a female lioness pawing a lionete to the right.

Cangzhen and Changgeng respectively.

**Palace of Heavenly Purity** This is the main palace in the Inner Court. It is a great hall with nine bays, 49 m long, 21.5 m wide and 24 m high. An imperial throne was placed in it. The hall has been restored and renovated several times since it was built up in 1421 (19th year of the reign of the Ming Emperor Yongle). The Palace of Heavenly Purity was restored in the reign of Emperor Jiaqing in the Qing Dynasty.

The furnishings in front of the palace are similar to those in front of the Hall of Supreme Harmony, but the layout of buildings around the palace is different. It has no side halls in front, but is flanked by two smaller halls. Attached at the eastern side is the Hall of Luminous Benevolence, while to its west is the Hall of Glorifying Virtue.

**Pavilion of Land and Grain Fronting the Palace of Heavenly Purity**

The Pavilion of Land and Grain is a square gilded bronze structure with a double-eaved roof. The conical upper part and square lower part of the roof imply the concept that the heavens are round and the earth is square. The pavilion sits on a three-tiered stone base. The upper tier is decorated with patterns of sea waves and river banks. In ancient ages, the combination of land and Grain symbolized the political power of a state.

**Tripod in front of the Palace of Heavenly Purity**

The Palace of Heavenly Purity served as the residence of the emperor, and thus the structure and its surrounding are of the highest rank, similar to the Hall of supreme Harmony. Tripods sitting in front of both palatial buildings symbolize the land and state.

The Palace of Heavenly Purity was a place where the Ming and Qing emperors used to reside and conduct state affairs.

**Hall of Union** The Hall of Union is similar to the Hall of Complete Harmony in form and style, but much smaller. It is a square, three-bayed building, with a pyramidal roof. In the Qing Dynasty, the Hall of Union was the place where the imperial concubines and imperial princes saluted the empress on festive occasions, such as the Lunar New Year's Day, the Thousand-Year's Day (the birthday of the empress), and so on.

**Palace of Earthly Tranquility** The Palace of Earthly Tranquility is similar to the Palace of Heavenly Purity in form and style, but somewhat smaller, being 45.5 m long and 17 m wide. It used to be the residence of the empresses in the Ming Dynasty. Heavenly purity combined with earthly tranquility would make the world pure and tranquil, which meant that the country would be at peace and the empire would reign forever and ever. Since the early Ming Dynasty in Nanjing and Beijing, it was still the practice to name the residences of the emperor and empress as the Palaces of Heavenly Purity and Earthly Tranquility. The exterior and interior of the palaces, however, were changed by the Qing Court according to Manchurian habit. In 1656 (13th year of Emperor Shunzhi), the Palace of Earthly Tranquility was changed radically after the style of the Manchu palace in Shenyang.

**Interior of the Hall of Manifest Harmony**

The Hall of Manifest Harmony was rebuilt in the mid-Qing period and was used as a dining hall for Empress Dowager Cixi when she was residing in the Palace of Gathering Excellence. Empress Dowager Cixi selected empress and imperial concubines for Emperor Guangxu in the hall in 1887.

**Palace of Gathering Excellence**

The Palace of Gathering Excellence built in 1420, was originally known as the Palace of Longevity and Prosperity, with the present name introduced in 1535.

**East Six and West Six Palaces** Each palace was built on a lot, each side 50 m long, forming a quadrangle with a well inside and a walled enclosure around it. As a rule, the entrance to the palace is situated on the south side at its centre. Two halls stand on the central axis of the quadrangle; the front hall was used as a living room, and the rear hall, as a bedroom. There are suites of rooms on the two sides for the attendants. Behind the side buildings, there is a lane for night watching. The layout of a palace is basically the same as that of the courtyards of common people in Beijing. The front halls in these palaces are usually built of five bays with a gable-

**Bridal Chamber in the Palace of Earthly Tranquility**

The East Warm Chamber in the Palace of Earthly Tranquility served as the imperial bridal chamber, and the palace was the residence of the empress during the Ming Dynasty. During the Qing Dynasty, the western section of the palace was used as a slaughterhouse and venue for sacrificial ceremonies and was thus unsuitable as a residence for the empress. Nonetheless, the Qing Court continued to recognize the palace as the formal residence of the empress. The palace continued to house the bridal chamber and was the venue for wedding banquets.

**Section of the Qing Painting titled Wedding of Emperor Guangxu**

Top right: Gate of Great Qing.
Lower right: Guards of honor on the terrace and flight of steps in front of the Hall of Supreme Harmony offer their congratulations.
Left: Palace of Compassion and Tranquility.

**Gate of Following Righteousness** / left

The Gate of Following Righteousness serves as entrance from the first long alley to the palatial complex in the Hall of Mental Cultivation. A screen wall, which sits just inside the gate on the opposite side, is decorated with glazed ornaments.

**Entrance to the Palace of Eternal Spring** / right

The entrance gate to the Palace of Eternal Spring, an imitation wood frame structure, is a glazed structure with a Sumeru base, a design similar to that of the Gate of Imperial Supremacy. The Palace of Eternal Spring is one of the west six palaces. The Hall of Manifest Harmony sits to the south and the complex of the Palace of Complete Happiness sits to the north.

and-hipped roof, except the Palace in the northeast of the East Six Palaces and the Xianfu Palace of Jingyang in the northwest of the West Six Palaces. These two buildings are both of three bays, with a hipped roof. The palaces are separated by crisscross alleys. The north-south alleys are 9 or 7 m wide, the east-west alleys, 4 m only. Gates are located at the ends.

**Hall of Mental Cultivation** Emperor Yongzheng observed a period of mourning for his father, the late Emperor Kangxi, in the Hall of Mental Cultivation. He continued to live there even after the mourning had long ended. Thereafter, the later emperors continued to use the Hall of Mental Cultivation as a place to conduct state affairs. The plan of the hall is in a shape of Chinese character "工". In the centre of its front hall, an imperial throne was placed with a golden dragon caisson ceiling above. Hence, the Hall of Mental Cultivation had the same function as the Palace of Heavenly Purity. The West Warm Chamber, located in the west side of the hall, used to be the place for Emperor Yongzheng and the later emperors to receive higher officials of the Grand Council. On the west end of the hall, the Room of the Three Rarities is located, where Emperor Qianlong kept three rare models of calligraphy, i.e. *the Kuaixue Shiqing Copybook by Wang Xizhi of the Jin period, the Mid-Autumn Copybook by his son Wang Xianzhi, and the Boyuan Copybook by Wang Xun.* The East Warm Chamber, located in the east side of the hall, where the Empress Dowager Cixi together with the Empress Dowager Ci'an practiced her "conducting state affairs from behind the yellow curtain" (Cixi conveyed her decisions on state affairs from behind the curtain to the six-year-old Emperor Tongzhi sitting on the throne in front).

**East Five and West Five Lodges** The lodges, located to the north of the East Six and West Six Palaces, used to be the residences of the imperial princes. Each lodge was a three-courtyard quadrangle with a well and a walled enclosure, north-south 55 m long, and east-west 27 to 30 m long. The first courtyard

**Panoramic View of the Nine-Dragon Screen Inside the Gate of Imperial Supremacy**

The Nine-Dragon Screen, a glazed screen wall decorated with nine glazed dragons, sits opposite the gate of Imperial Supremacy.

Gate of Spiritual Cultivation

The Gate of Spiritual Cultivation serves as the entrance to the northern section of the Palace of Tranquil Longevity complex.

consisted of a main hall and two side suites of rooms; the second courtyard was the same as the first; the third had only the north suite of rooms. The entrance to the lodge was located at the centre of the south wall of the quadrangle. The lodge was similar in form and style to the quadrangle of common people in Beijing.

**Palace of Tranquil Longevity** This palatial complex is located in the northeast of the Forbidden City. It was rebuilt on the site of a Ming palace in 1699 (38th year of Emperor Kangxi), and extended in 1772 (37th year of Emperor Qianlong). Emperor Qianlong had been planning to live in this palace in case he abdicated. In fact, only rambling about here occasionally, he never lived in the palace even after his abdication.

The entrance to the palatial complex was named the Gate of Imperial Supremacy. Opposite the gate there stands a screen wall, which was clad in coloured glazed tiles with a design of nine molded dragons, known as the Nine-Dragon Screen. The front hall of the palatial complex is called the Hall of Imperial Supremacy, 45 m long (east-west) and 20 m wide (north-south), with a form and size similar to the Palace of Heavenly Purity. It was erected on a high white stone terrace with an elevated way in front, leading to the Gate of

Tranquil Longevity. The rear hall is the Palace of Tranquil Longevity, modelled after the Palace of Earthly Tranquility. Therefore, in the west part of the hall, a place for sacrificial ceremonies was laid out, while its east part was no longer a bridal chamber, but a bedroom.

**Palace of Compassion and Tranquility** This palatial complex is located in the west of the Forbidden City. When a grand ceremony was held in the Qing Court, the empress dowager would receive congratulations here. The palace was first built in 1536 (15th year of the Ming Emperor Jiajing). Destroyed by fire in the period of Emperor Wanli, it was reconstructed later. In 1769 (34th year of Emperor Qianlong), it was rebuilt again for celebration of the 80th birthday of the Emperor's mother. Around the Palace of Compassion and Tranquility, there are some smaller palatial buildings. All these buildings were used as the residences of empress and concubines of the late emperor.

### 4. Gardens

There used to be four gardens in the Forbidden City. The Garden of the Palace for the Establishment of Happiness, built in 1740 (5th year of Emperor Qianlong), was entirely destroyed by fire in 1933. The other three gardens still exist: the Imperial Garden, the Garden of the Palace of Tranquil Longevity and the Garden of the Palace of Compassion and Tranquility.

**Imperial Garden** This was originally called the "Back Garden of the Palace" during the Ming Dynasty. Built at the same time as the Ming palaces and halls, it still retains its original character and layout, though it has experienced many restorations and renovations. Many buildings, trees and rockery hills in the garden have survived from the early Ming Dynasty. The garden is 140 m east-west, and 80 m north-south. Buildings and structures were arranged and coordinated for symmetrical balance on the central axis of the Forbidden City. Such a symmetrical layout can hardly be found in traditional gardens in China. On the northern end of the central axis is the main hall of the garden, which is the Hall of Imperial Peace. To the east are the Hall of Piled Excellence, the Hall of Literary Elegance, the Jade-Green Floating Pavilion, the Pavilion of Ten Thousand Springs, the Pavilion of Red Snow, etc. Correspondingly to the west are the Pavilion of Prolonged Sunshine, the Weiyu Study, the Pavilion of Auspicious Clarity, the Pavilion of One Thousand Autumns, the Studio of Spiritual Cultivation. Most of the buildings are set against the enclosed walls of the garden. In its central area, trees and flowers

**Pavilion of Ten Thousand Springs**

The Pavilion of Ten Thousand Springs, in the centre of the eastern section of the Imperial Garden, was built in1536. The fact that the upper level of the two-tiered roof is conical and lower level is square alludes to the concept that the heaven is round and the earth is square.

**Corridor in the Western Garden of the Palace of Tranquil Longevity**

A corridor to the west of the Study of Peaceful Old Age provides access to the Pavilion of the Anticipation of Good Fortune. A curved courtyard wall with glazed decorative openwork windows sits to the west of the corridor. The Hall of Bamboo Fragrance, an elegant two-storey building, sits in the courtyard.

are planted, small pavilions and platforms are scattered, and fantastic rocks with miniature trees and rockery are displayed.

**Garden of the Palace of Compassion and Tranquility** It measures more than 50 m east-west and about 130 m north-south. It was first built in the Ming Dynasty and renovated in the Qing period, with a symmetrical plan. On its central axis, there are the Pavilion of the Brookside in the south and the Xianruo Buddhist Hall in the north. Behind the Buddhist Hall is the Building of Compassionate Shelter. To the east and west of the Buddhist Hall are the Building of Buddha's Features and the Building of Auspicious Clouds. Images of Buddhas and Buddhist scriptures were housed here. In the reign of Emperor

**Pavilion of Pleasant Sounds**

The Pavilion of Pleasant Sounds, located to the east of the Hall of Spiritual Cultivation, was a venue for the theatrical performance. The pavilion was originally built in 1772 and was rebuilt in 1819. The performance area consists of three floors, each of which has a stage. The stage on the lower floor, or the main stage and largest of the three, was known as the Stage of Longevity. The intermediate floor was known as the Stage of Good Fortune, and the upper floor as the Stage of Happiness. Large-scale plays featuring hundreds of actors simultaneously performing on all three stages formed an exciting scene of "immortals congratulating the emperor or empress on his or her birthday" or "the Land of Ultimate Bliss".

Qianlong, the Study of Embodiment of Purity and the Hall of Extended Long Life were built in front of the Buddhist Hall on the east and west sides. Emperor Qianlong used to live there to wait upon and to look after his diseased mother with decocted medicine, and later to observe a period of mourning after her death.

**Garden of the Palace of Tranquil Longevity** This garden was built in 1771 (36th year of Emperor Qianlong). It was built on a narrow lot, 160 m north-south, but only 37 m east-west. There are five courtyards laid out on the garden site.

## 5. Theatrical Stages

The Pavilion of Pleasant Sounds is the largest theatrical performing place in the Forbidden City. It is a storeyed building in the shape of the Chinese character "凸". The front part is the performing area, with three storeys each being a stage. The upper storey is called the Stage of Happiness, the middle one Stage of Good Fortune, and the lower one Stage of Longevity.

**Hall of Abstinence**

The Hall of Abstinence, built in 1731, is located east of the Palace of Heavenly Purity. Early Qing emperors fasted in the hall before journeying to the southern suburbs to offer sacrifices to the Heaven, to the northern suburbs to offer sacrifices to Earth and to offer sacrifices to the Gods of Land and Grain on the Winter Solstice.

**Interior of the Xianruo Buddhist Hall**

The Xianruo Buddhist Hall is located in the Garden of the Palace of Compassion and Tranquility. The hall was set aside exclusively as a venue for the empress dowager and concubines to worship Buddha. The hall houses an array of Buddhist statues, sacrificial objects and musical instruments.

The Stages of Happiness and Good Fortune are relatively small, especially with less depth. They were designed according to the angle of vision of the emperor sitting on the throne in Yueshilou Building, the imperial building opposite the stages for the emperor to watch operas. To the east and west are viewing galleries for princes, dukes and ministers. All decorative paintings and ornaments for the Pavilion of Pleasant Sounds are splendid.

### 6. Buddhist and Taoist Halls and Other Places of Worship

There were many halls and buildings in the Forbidden City serving as places of religious worship for the imperial family. Although Lamaism became the state religion during the Qing Dynasty, Taoism and Confucianism retained their traditional importance. Hence some worship halls of the Ming Court were preserved.

The extant Taoist halls were mainly built in the Ming Dynasty. The Hall of Imperial Peace is a relatively special building. Its roof is truncated-hipped. A roof of this kind was first recorded in the Yuan Dynasty. Incense burners and ceramic tiled ovens for burning sacrificial offerings, as well as flagpoles

**Panoramic View of the Inner Golden River**

The Inner Golden River flows from the west into the Forbidden City. The name Inner Golden River is derived from the fact that the west stands for metal or gold, part of the five elements. The river flows through the Forbidden City and exits the complex in the southeast corner. The Inner Golden River, the main water source of the Forbidden City, supplies water for both fire protection and civil engineering projects. The river is also used for drainage, with rainwater flowing into drainage system through open troughs or underground drains. Water then flows into the main underground drainage system and enters the inner golden river over a spillway on a vertical revetment.

decorated with dragon-cloud designs, were erected in front of the Hall of Imperial Peace.

In the Forbidden City, there are a number of Buddhist buildings including halls, pavilions etc. Most of them are in the living quarters of the empress and concubine dowagers, such as the Hall of Exuberance, located to the north of the Palace of Tranquil Old Age. It was a five-bay hall with a three-bay small hall attached to each of its side walls, built in the Ming Dynasty and renovated in the periods of Kangxi and Qianlong of the Qing Dynasty. The Nine-Lotus Boddhisattva was enshrined and worshipped here. The mother of Ming Emperor Wanli once dreamed of the Nine-Lotus Boddhisattva imparting Buddhist scriptures to her. Hence, in the light of the story of Sakyamuni, she planted two bodhi trees in front of the hall. It was under the bodhi trees,

**Detailed View of the Inner Golden River** / left

Five white marble bridges span the Inner Golden River which is symmetrically laid out in the courtyard in front of the Gate of Supreme Harmony. The river meanders through the Forbidden City both above and below ground. The design creates a splendid and artistic atmosphere for the Forbidden City.

**Zhenfei Well** / right

The well is located inside the Gate of Truth and Compliance in the Palace of Tranquil Longevity complex. Zhenfei, an imperial concubine of Emperor Guangxu, drowned in the well. Her death came at the hands of Cui Yugui, a eunuch who acted on the orders of Empress Dowager Cixi when the Eight-Power Allied Forces invaded Beijing.

Sakyamuni attained enlightenment and became Buddha. Now the two trees have deep roots and luxuriant leaves with a height of more than six m. In late autumn, their seeds may be used to make a rosary of strung beads.

### 7. Services

**Water Supply and Drainage** The water source of the moat and the golden river of the Forbidden city lies in the Yuquan (Jade Spring Hill) in the western suburbs of Beijing. The moat enters the Forbidden City at its northwest corner through a culvert beneath the city wall, emerging inside the city as the inner golden river. It flows southward along the western side of the city, and then, turns east, passing in front of the Gate of Military Eminence, across the courtyard in front of the Gate of Supreme Harmony and through the imperial library. Finally, it turns south and flows out from the city at its southeastern corner. Its entire course is more than 2,000 m in length, passing under more than 20 bridges and through some 10 culverts.

Liu Ruoyu, a eunuch of the Ming Court, in his book *the History of the Ming Palace* writes that this river is not for enjoying the fish swimming in the water plants, but for putting out the fire and other accidents, as well as supplying water for construction. The water of the pools in the Imperial Garden and the Garden of the Palace of Compassion and Tranquility is also drawn from the inner golden river. In fact, the inner golden river played the most important role in supplying water to the court.

**East Warm Chamber in the Hall of Mental Cultivation**

Empress Dowager Cixi gained power after a palace coup d'etat in 1861. Thereafter, she introduced the practice of "conducting state affairs from behind yellow curtains", i.e. Cixi sat behind the curtain and conveyed her decisions on state affairs to Emperor Tongzhi, and later to Emperor Guangxu who sat on the throne seat in front. The east chamber was warm in winter and cool in summer. In winter, fires were lit in the outdoor heating pit under the front eaves and heated air flowing through brick ducts would heat the indoor brick floor. The floor was usually covered with carpets or rugs and a number of braziers were placed throughout the room, hence the name Warm Chamber.

**Heating and Heat Insulation** On the 1st day of the 11th lunar month every year, known as the "Stove Lighting Day", stoves were lit and the hollow brick beds were warmed by fire from below. However, the date was not strictly defined. The Archives of the Qing Court records that the coal for heating the places where the emperor and empress lived were prepared on the last ten days of the 9th lunar month every year, for it had been much colder at that time.

Heating in the palace was usually by a fire lit in a pit or flue built beneath the floor. Heating pits were constructed on the platform of the hall or palace in the veranda under its front eaves. The pit was about 1.5 m deep with a manhole covered with a plank lid on the floor level of the platform. Brick ducts and flues were built turning round beneath the floor and the brick bed surface. When the fire was lit, heated air would go through the brick ducts to the exterior outlet, warming the floor and the brick bed. Rooms in the halls or palaces equipped with such a heating system are called "warm chambers".

**Daylight and Illumination** Though a palatial hall usually has windows both in front and in the rear, it is hard to let in enough daylight due to the depth of the hall and the lattice decorations of the windows. Especially in the early years, the windows could only be pasted with sheets of paper, for there was no glass for glazing. Therefore, the interior space of the hall could not help being dark. In the period of Emperor Kangxi, glass was first used in an imperial garden in the western suburbs of the capital. Emperors Qianlong and Jiaqing both had some pieces of poems relating to the window glass. It showed that glass had never been used in the Forbidden City until their reigns.

When night came, candles were the only source of illumination in the Forbidden City. The candles were made exquisite with gilded dragon designs on the surface. A candle with a shade made of goat horn strips and pasted with gauze is referred to as a lamp or a lantern. Among the lamps and lanterns used in the Forbidden City, some are placed on tables or desks known as table lanterns; some are suspended from ceilings or eaves known as pendent lanterns; some called stand lanterns are those standing on indoor floors; some called street lamps are those placed on stone stands standing outdoors. As these lamps and lanterns caught fire easily, lighting regulations in the Imperial Courts were extremely strict. There were no definite places to set up lanterns in the outer court. Going to court before dawn, only the princes were allowed to light the way with lanterns to the Gate of Great Fortune or the Gate of the Great Ancestors. Higher officials of the Grand Council were allowed to take goat-horn lanterns to enter the right inner gate. The rest had to walk without any light. However, the emperor had lanterns in pairs hung from dragon-head poles in front and corner lamps in the rear. The goat-horn lanterns would be placed in front of the imperial throne on its two sides when the morning court was held in winter.

## III. Architectural Construction and Decoration

Based on the historical background of Chinese civilization, Chinese architecture has developed an entirely complete and independent system. It has its own conventions, standardized form and style, as well as official and local construction methods. Palace architecture requires an official construction method strictly confined to form and style. An account of the main parts of the architectural construction in the Forbidden City is dealt with as follows.

### 1. Terraces and Platforms

A distinguishing feature of the palace architecture is the terrace where a building or a building complex stands. Several ancient palatial building sites have been unearthed to reveal that they were all erected on large scaled rammed-earth terraces. In the Spring and Autumn Period, it was not unusual for state rulers (dukes or princes) to compete with one another to "make the terrace higher and the palace more decorative". In the Qin and Han dynasties, the high-terraced buildings developed to the highest stage. Buildings erected on large and high rammed-earth terraces were designed to prevent from dampness, offering advantages in ventilation and convenience in defense, as well as being of magnificent appearance. Although this practice underwent some changes in later dynasties, the height of the terrace was still the important symbol of social position of the occupants in the Ming and Qing dynasties. *The Collected Statutes of the Qing Dynasty* records, "For position of a nobleman lower than duke or marquis, or for that of an official higher than third rank, the height of the platform, or terrace, of the building should be two Chinese feet. For the position of an official lower than fourth rank, or for common people, it should be one Chinese foot." The highest ranking halls built in the period of the Ming Emperor Yongle, such as the three great halls in the Forbidden City, the Hall of Prayer for Good Harvest in the Temple of Heaven, and the Hall of Heavenly Favors in the Ming Tombs, were all erected on three-tiered terraces with Sumeru

**Partition Doors in the Palace of Heavenly Purity** / left

Decorations on the partition doors of exterior fittings mainly focused on the decorative patterns on lattice sashes and panels. Lattice sashes on partition doors in the Palace of Heavenly Purity featured water chestnut trellis patterns with bars in three directions. The panels were decorated with round glided dragons and floating clouds. Bronzed plates and angles for fastening stiles and rails were all gilded and engraved with dragon motifs. All decorations were made in the highest ranking decorations.

**Partition Doors in the Hall of Imperial Supremacy** / middle

A partition door is composed of a lattice sash, two or three strip panels and a skirt panel framed by two vertical stiles and five or six horizontal rails.

**Partition Panels in the Hall of Supreme Harmony** / right

Gilded bronze angles in the magnificent palaces were often nailed on joints where rails intersected with stiles. They were not only used for decoration, but also for fastening door frames.

bases. Sumeru, or Mount Meru, was a fabled mountain in ancient India, which was considered the cosmic centre of Buddhism. The three-tiered terrace where the Three Great Halls are located is 8.13 m high, in the shape of the Chinese character "工". The three tiers of the terrace, laid one upon the other, are all surrounded by white marble balustrades with upright stone posts in between. In the central part of the flights of steps and along their slope, are large marble slabs carved with patterns of dragon or the dragon-phoenix in various postures, referred to as the "imperial way stones".

## 2. Exterior Finish Work

Doors, windows and the like located under the eaves or exposed outdoors are classified in Chinese architecture as the "outer eave fittings", or "exterior finish". In timber-framed structures, columns are the main vertical structural members to carry the loads from the roof, while the walls are non-load bearing. Doors and windows are all fitted in between the columns, forming an important factor in the facades. Doors and windows under the front eaves of a hall are usually installed between the hypostyle columns, which are columns in the second line, just next to the peristyle columns, forming a verandah of the hall in front. Some halls also have doors and windows between the rear hypostyle columns, where the verandahs are both in the front and rear. Some halls have verandahs of this kind on the four sides.

Partition doors and silled windows are specially used in principal palaces and halls. A partition door is composed of a latticed sash, a skirt panel and one or three strip panels, framed by two vertical stiles and several horizontal rails. Decorations are mainly on the latticed sash and panels. Water chestnut trellis patterns with bars in two or three directions are the highest ranking lattice work used on the sash of the partition door. "Step-by-step" (bu bu jin) patterns and "lantern frame" patterns are the next.

### 3. Timber Frames and Bracket Sets

Timber frame construction in beam-column type is commonly adopted in buildings in the Forbidden City. The beam-column timber frames are constructed as follows. The columns are erected on stone bases. Carried on columns and spanning the depth of the building, a series of beams are arranged one above another with diminishing lengths. The upper beam is supported on short posts under each end to the beam below. The short posts are of different lengths, the lower the shorter, thus forming the curved roof. As for the hipped, gable-and-hipped, and gabled roofs, only some specific alterations are made in the two end bays.

**Bracket Sets Under the Eaves on the Gate of Mid-Left**

Structural bracket sets were an integral part of the timber structures in ancient times. Bracket sets were often simple and large. However, they were somewhat smaller and more decorative during the Ming and Qing dynasties.

Bracket sets are wood members supporting the roofs and the overhanging eaves. The bracket system originated in very early times. It might be said that it was developed together with the Chinese civilization. It matured in the Tang Dynasty. Since then, it appeared more decorative. In the feudal dynasties, the bracket system could only be used in imperial palaces and temples, as it is remarked, "It is not allowed to place bracket sets and caissons, unless the house is an imperial palace."

A set of brackets consists of four basic members. They are the arm-shaped members extending out from the facade of the building called "qiao", the bow-shaped members supported by qiao and parallel to the building facade called "gong", the blocks placed beneath or between qiao and gong called "dou" (main block) or "sheng"(secondary blocks), and the slanting members like birds' beaks in place of qiao called "ang". The qiao may be used in successive tiers, each extending out a certain distance, called a "tiao", or a "jump". Bracket sets may be classified into a variety of kinds according to the number of "jumps" and the size of their component members. The bracket sets used in the Hall of Supreme Harmony are of the highest rank. Those under its upper eaves are the four-jump sets, while under the lower eaves, they are three-jump sets. Bracket sets in other halls are all in relatively smaller number of jumps. In the side halls, galleries and corridors, bracket sets usually have no jumps, only a main block and two or three secondary blocks joined by an arm or gong, located on the centre line of the exterior or peristyle columns. Such arrangement was not only to show the ranks or positions of the buildings, but also to meet architectural requirements. It is mechanically and proportionally rational that the taller a building, the more the overhang of its eaves, the more the jumps of its bracket sets.

### 4. Types of Roof

A prominent feature of Chinese architecture is its beautiful and gigantic roofs. As the palatial halls are larger than usual buildings, their roofs are more conspicuous. The hipped roof is the earliest roof form recorded in ancient literature. *The Survey on Construction Work in the Ritual of Zhou* records, "Yin people have halls with roofs double-eaved and four-sloped." Here Yin refers to the Shang Dynasty (c. 16th~11th c BC) and four-sloped means hipped. In the long history of feudal society in China, this verse was considered as a rule for building the most respected halls. Sometimes, buildings were built with roofs hipped but single-eaved.

**Glazed Roof Ornaments on the Hall of Supreme Harmony**

The lower ends of sloping ridges on palatial halls were usually decorated with a series of small mythological figures. The following sequence of figures gradually formed over time: the lower, or the first, figure at the ridge end depicted a celestial prince on the back of a hen, followed in an upward direction by a dragon, phoenix, lion, celestial horse, sea-horse, suanni, yayu, xiezhi, and douniu. The Hall of Supreme Harmony was of the highest rank, and thus another figure, the xingshi, was added at the highest level of the sequence.

Slightly lower in rank than the hipped roof is the gable-and-hipped roof with a double or single tier of eaves. It is formed by a gabled roof with gablets placed over a hipped roof. The ancient paintings show that many halls, including palatial halls, of the Song Period were of gable-and-hipped roofs. A hall with a roof of this kind was called a "nine-ridged hall" in the Song Period, for it has nine ridges: a horizontal one on the top, four sloping ones at the two gablets, and four diagonal ones at the corners. Gable-and-hipped roofs are used in tall and important buildings, such as the Gate of Heavenly Peace, Gate of Correct Demeanor, Gate of Supreme Harmony, Hall of Preserving Harmony, Palace of Tranquil Longevity, Palace of Compassion and Tranquility, etc.

The next form of roofs is the gabled roof with or without overhangs at its two sides. Besides, there are some other roof forms. The pyramidal roof is usually used to cover a square pavilion. Some buildings combine several different roof forms.

There is also a form of roof which is truncated pyramidal or truncated-hipped. The roof of the Hall of Imperial Peace in the Imperial Garden belongs to this category.

The decorations of the roofs are plentiful and colourful. Many mythological interpretations are attached to them. In fact, most of these decorations are essential structural elements with artistic treatments.

A ridge is constructed by laying tiles on the junction of two roof-slopes to protect it from rain seepage. The ends of the horizontal ridge need to be protected for this is the point where the horizontal ridge meets the two sloping ridges. Hence a finial is placed there. The original form of the finial was a fish tail, later on it became a bird's tail. In the Ming and Qing periods, the finial became a dragon, holding the ridge end in its mouth with a sword implanted in its back. At the eave-corners, the diagonal ridges are reinforced by a series of small mythological figures, the first one at the ridge end being a hen with

**Exterior Ceiling in the Hall of Spiritual Cultivation**

The coffered ceiling is composed of joists and ceiling boards. Decorative paintings, mainly in blue and green, are painted on both elements. Ceiling boards are decorated with central blue roundel with dragon motifs. The four corners of the boards and the cruciform joints of the joists are painted in the same colour.

a celestial prince astride, and then, moving upwards, dragon, phoenix, lion, celestial horse, sea-horse, suanni (a beast of prey), yayu, xiezhi (a fabulous animal reputed to be able to distinguish between good and evil), and douniu. A roof pommel, usually made of gilt bronze, is used to cover the top of a pyramidal or conical roof to protect the king-post of the timber frame against the weather.

### 5. Interior Finish Work

Interior finish, classified as the "inner eave fittings" in Chinese architecture, includes the partitions, screens and the members used to separate the interior spaces, ceilings, and so on.

The immovable interior walls are usually built of bricks or wood panels pasted with paper sheets. The latter is known as a wood-board partition. Partition doors and screens are movable partitions which may be made open or

**Coffered Ceiling in the Pavilion of Ancient Flowers**

While the coffered ceiling in the Pavilion of Ancient Flowers retains its original wood grain without colour paintings. Its surfaces are carved in patterns with plant motifs.

**Caisson Ceiling in the Pavilion of One Thousand Autumns**

This is a round caisson consisting of two layers with a series of small bracket sets in between. The lower layer is surrounded by a ringed coffered ceiling with the boards decorated in double-phoenix patterns. The upper layer is a dome with a carved wooden coiled dragon suspended in the centre.

closed, or moved to separate various interior spaces. The most common type of interior finish work is the perforate ornamental partitioning screen, called "zhao", used in the residences of empress and imperial concubines in the inner court. It is an openwork curtain-like screen, suspended under the beam or across the ceiling, forming a space looking like it is separated but in reality not quite separated.

A partition made up of six, eight or ten partition doors placed in line with two doors in the middle, opening inward, is referred to as "bi sha chu" (literally, green-gauze cabinet). A partition of this kind is more exquisite than partition doors of the exterior finish work. The lattice sashes of these partition doors are usually of various types of "lantern-frame" patterns with glass inserted in between the outer and inner sashes, or, with paper or gauze pasted on the sashes. Sometimes calligraphy, painting or embroidery was made on the gauze or paper to enhance the tasteful atmosphere of the interior. On the stiles and rails of the partition doors, pieces of jade, shell or cloisonne, are usually inserted with various patterns.

There are a variety of perforate ornamental partitioning screens. Some are assembled with an overhanging frame and two partition doors fixed on either side. Some are composed of a suspended screen and balustrades on either side with an opening in the middle. Some are overall perforate ornamental wood-carved partitions with an opening, round, octagonal or other geometric form, in the middle. Some are made in front of the brick bed. Some are made to be shelves for antiques or to be bookshelves. Most of them are made of red sandalwood, rosewood or mahogany with extremely ornate fretwork of different motifs. Patterns of trailing plants as grapes or wisteria are commonly used in residences of imperial concubines to symbolize the prosperity of posterity. Patterns of magnolia, peony, bats and Buddhist swastikas are used there to imply happiness, good fortune and longevity. As for the ornamental partitioning screen in front of the brick bed, bright-coloured embroidered silk curtains are suspended in front, and wood cabinets are usually installed on either side of the bed.

The interior of the halls and palaces in the Forbidden City may be with or without ceilings. A building interior without ceilings was called "exposed roof-frame construction" in the Song Dynasty, for in these buildings all roof frames including purlins, rafters and bracket sets are exposed to the interior space. Several gate halls in the outer court were built without ceilings such as the Left and Right Back Gates, Gate of Great Ancestors, Gate of Luminous Virtue and Gate of Correct Conduct. Most buildings had ceilings to keep roof frames out of view.

Caissons, or "zao jing" (literally, decorative wells), were built in the ceilings of the most important buildings. A caisson is a dome-like structure assembled in the centre of a coffered ceiling. How did it come to be used in the ceilings? What was its function?

It was said that in the remote ages when people lived in caves, an opening for lighting and ventilation had to be made in the top of the cave where sacrificial offerings were held. As the opening appeared like a well and was decorated for its importance, hence it was called a decorative well. Whatever it meant, the caissons built in the halls of the Ming-Qing periods were mainly decorative.

The construction of caissons is very sophisticated. A caisson is usually composed of three parts: the upper, the intermediate and the lower, as in the Hall of Supreme Harmony. In the centre of the plate, there is a writhing dragon holding a pearl in its mouth, alluding to the Dragon in Heaven. Beneath it is the imperial throne where sat the Dragon on Earth, or the emperor. The two Dragons echoed each other, constituting such a sacred atmosphere that other decorations could never achieve.

**6. Decorative Painting**

In order to prevent the wood members from cracking, rot and insect pests, a protective coating made of powder paste and hemp fiber is applied to the surface of the wood members after which it is painted, thus making the hall or

**Xuanzi Decorative Painting Under the Eaves on the Gate of Mid-Right**

Xuanzi, or whirling flower, painting is lower than hexi painting in ranking. It is named for its zao tou, or intervening section, being decorated with a motif of whirling flowers called Xuanzi. The painting is divided into sections with bent lines. Xuanzi paintings fall into seven ranks according to the amount of gold used and the application of different colours. Blue and green are the main colours of Xuanzi paintings, with black, white and gold used for embellishment.

**Hexi Decorative Painting in the Palace of Tranquil Longevity**

Hexi decorative paintings are the highest rank, with golden-dragon patterned painting representing the highest level of nobility. Hexi paintings are divided into sections by double "W" lines. All lines and patterns are painted resplendently, with power dribbling and gold-leafing.

palace splendid in various colours.

Decorative painting was considerably matured in the Song Dynasty, and became conventional and standardized in the Ming and Qing periods. The styles and forms of it were strictly defined. In the Ming Dynasty, it was promulgated that common people were not allowed to decorate their dwelling houses with polychrome paintings, since then paintings of this kind related only to the imperial palaces and religious temples.

Decorative paintings used in the Forbidden City are divided into three categories: hexi, xuanzi and Su-style. Paintings of the three categories are mainly in green and blue, and are all composed of three parts: "fang xin" ( the central part), "gu tou" (hooped ends) and "zhao tou" or "zao tou" (intervening part). In light of the application of the three categories to the halls and palaces, hexi painting is highest in rank. The important halls and palaces in the outer and inner courts were all decorated with hexi paintings, whose design and layout were strictly regulated. Motifs of patterns of hexi painting are all dragons and phoenixes in varied and lively postures. In the Hall of Supreme Harmony, there is a beam, on which 20 dragons are painted with powder dribbling and goldleafing in a large area. Hexi paintings in dragon and phoenix motifs are applied to the Palace of Earthly Tranquility, East and West Six Palaces, etc. Those in dragon and grass motifs are applied to the Gate of Correct Demeanor, Meridian Gate, Pavilion of Manifest Benevolence, etc.

## IV. Construction Work

In 1406 (4th year of Ming Emperor Yongle) Zhu Di (the emperor's real name) issued an imperial edict to build the imperial palace, ancestral temple and altars in Beijing, as well as his own tomb at Changling, in the mountains some 45 kms northwest of the capital. The preparation work was to start in the next year. After planning and ample preparations, construction work formally began in the 2nd lunar month of 1417 (15th year of Yongle), and was completed in the 11th lunar month of 1420. The imperial palace was formally used on Lunar New Year's Day 1421.

Such a huge construction project was completed in less than four years. It cannot be overemphasized that the preparations were adequate and the building process had been organized scientifically.

In the field of building technology, some simple machines, such as manual hoist, jack, etc. had come into use to enhance working efficiency. Timber-framed structures had experienced a period of change, but had basically become standardized by the Ming Dynasty. As for the design and construction of imperial buildings, the Qing Court established two separate departments: the Modeling House in charge of building design and the Reckoning House in charge of construction budgeting. A concrete system of estimating labor and materials, as well as the checking and examination of construction works, was formed. Extant drawings and models of buildings and building complexes, kept for several hundred years, have fully proved that the designs were worked out after careful consideration.

In the Ming Dynasty, the majority of city walls in the country, as well as the main part of the Great Wall, were all faced with bricks. A great number of bricks were used in local construction works. Glazed tiles made of a clay base became more colourful, along with numerous patterns and greater hardness.

## 1. Organization of Construction

The Ming Court set up the Board of Works. Under it, there was the Building and Repairing Department in charge of construction affairs, and under it, in turn, was the Building and Repair Office. In the Qing Court, the Board of Works continued to exist, but the building and repairing of imperial palaces and gardens were handled by the Board of Domestic Affairs.

From the historical records on the building process of the Forbidden City, it is evident that Wu Zhong, the construction director, who was also the head of the Board of Works at the Court, and Cai Xin, a technician of the Building and Repairing Office, both had rich experience in construction and they directed the work scientifically.

**Timber Columns in the Hall of Complete Harmony**

Large quantities of timber were used in the construction of the Forbidden City. Nanmu, the highest quality hardwood, was used in the construction of important buildings in the Forbidden City. The task of felling and transporting timber to Beijing was an arduous job carried out by a large contingent of forced laborers. The well-proportioned peristyle columns in the Hall of Complete Harmony, all of which are equal in size, were fashioned from red sandalwood. Although the columns are somewhat mottled, one can still imagine the vast amount of manpower and material resources involved the construction effort.

**Imperial Way Stone Slabs Leading to the Rear Terrace of the Hall of Preserving Harmony**

Flights of steps with ramps in between, both front and rear, lead to the three-tiered terrace and the three great halls, just on the central axis. Flanked by stone steps, the central parts of the flights are ramps laid with large carved marble slabs, forming the Imperial Way. The largest and most perfect marble slab carved with a design of precious hills and floating clouds, or "nine dragons playing with a pearl", is found on the imperial way behind the Hall of Preserving Harmony.

**Glazed Screen Wall Beside the Gate of Tranquil Longevity**

The brick screen wall sits on a white stone Sumeru base and is topped by a overhanging glazed-tiled roof. Glazed purlins, brackets sets and lintels sit bellow the eaves. The centre of the wall is decorated with a glazed oblate ornament, with a glazed triangular ornament on each corner.

Traditional methods for building city walls were to build the wall and excavate the moat at the same time. The excavated earth from the moat was then rammed to form an earthen city wall. As for the Forbidden City, the city walls were all faced with thick brickwork, hence, it did not need so much earth. The earth excavated from the moat, as well as that from the West Imperial Lake, was carried north of the Forbidden City to create the Prospect Hill, constituting an artificial environment of "hills behind and water in front", which was believed to be of high geomantic quality.

When the construction of the imperial palace started, the Grand Canal and the Tonghui River (a canal from Tongzhou to Beijing) had been dredged for shipping materials from South China. The Board of Works had set up five large storehouses for storing and processing materials. These were the Sacred Timber House, Great Timber House, Platform House, Black Kiln House and Glazed Tile House. Meanwhile, several working places had been laid outside the site of the Forbidden City for prefabricating wood and stone members. Since the Tang, and more especially, the Song Dynasty, the initial modular system had been applied to building design and construction. Wood members, stone blocks and brickworks were all proportioned in definite sizes. In case the basic dimensions of a building had been determined, which meant that the sizes of most of its members had been decided, these members might be prefabricated and sent to the building site where they would be assembled. Thus, the fact that such an enormous project could be finished relatively quickly is an unprecedented architectural phenomenon. This was partly due to the labor of over a million workers and the ingenuity and collaboration of the 100,000 planners and craftsmen who had been drafted from all parts of the country.

**2. Preparation of Materials**

When it was decided to build the Forbidden City, ministers and higher officials were sent to the provinces of Sichuan, Huguang, Jiangxi, Zhejiang and Shanxi to select timber. Nanmu, the best of all hardwoods, was usually used for frames as well as decorations in the Ming halls. The task of felling the trees and transporting them to Beijing, some 1,500 km away, was an arduous job. First, the logs were rolled down into the mountain gullies, where they were lashed together to form rafts. These were left to await for mountain torrents, which would carry the rafts down to the mountainside, and into the rivers. Via a network of waterways, most of the rafts eventually reached the Yangtze River. These timber rafts were then transported along the Grand Canal to Tongzhou, and again along the Tonghui River to the Sacred Timber House in Beijing.

As the selection of timber started, the production of bricks and tiles also began. The construction of the Forbidden City wanted an enormous amount of bricks and tiles. It is estimated that for the city walls, palace walls and the three-tiered terrace, 80 million bricks were required. Moreover, courtyards were paved with at least three layers of bricks, so that for the courtyards alone 20 million bricks were used. The aforementioned bricks are all large-sized and commonly-used, called "ting ni cheng zhuan" (literally, stopping-mud city-wall bricks). There were some other types needed in a large amount. Those used for finishing the wall surfaces were called "deng jiang zhuan" (literally, settled-clay bricks) and those square in shape for paving the interior floors were called "jin zhuan" (literally, metal bricks). One can well imagine what an astonishing quantity of bricks have been used in building the imperial palaces.

The square bricks for paving the floors of the main halls were produced in Suzhou. They were named "metal bricks" for they resounded like metal when struck. A book written by an official of the Ming Court in charge of the metal brick production in Suzhou states that it took 130 days for baking the bricks in kiln.

The glazed tiles used for covering roofs were manufactured in the Glazed Tile House originally located to the southwest, outside the South-Facing Gate.

Black tiles, or unglazed clay tiles, were produced in the Black Kiln House, which is now in Taoranting Park. The low-lying pieces of land left by excavation for fetching clay filled with water to form several lakes in the park.

The stones used in the Forbidden City were both great in number and huge in size. In the early Ming Dynasty, high standards were also set for their selection. For example, the length of the stone slabs covering the edge of the platform had to match the length of the bays. The length of the central bay of the Palace of Heavenly Purity measured 7 m, the length of the stone slab in front of the central bay also had to be 7 m. These stones were quarried from Da Shiwo (Big Stone Nest) in Fangshan and Qingbai Kou (Green-White Pass) in Mentougou, western Beijing. Stone of this kind, known for hardness and their green-white colour, were called "green-white marble" or "mugwort marble". Fangshan was also rich in white marble as white as snow, called "han bai yu" (literally, white jade of Han), which was widely used in the imperial palaces.

### 3. Famous Craftsmen

The planning and design of the imperial palaces must be examined first by the Board of Works. Then, it was sent to the emperor by a eunuch for approval. Extant archives of the Ming Court describes this procession. The archives record that three persons had done much work on the planning and design of the palace. They were Marquis Chen Gui, Wu Zhong, Chief of the Board of

**Balustrades in the Rear of the Hall of Imperial Peace**

Each panel on balustrades surrounding Hall of Imperial Peace is carved with a high relief pattern of "two dragons playing with a pearl", with the only exception being the panel on the central balustrade in the rear of the hall. This particular panel features carved sea waves with a distinct feature and perfect composition. The panel is an art treasure representing stone carvings used in palace architecture.'

**Dragon-Head Gargoyles on the Terrace of the Three Great Halls**

Gargoyles in the shape of the head of a chi, hornless dragon, are found directly beneath the stone posts of balustrades. The gargoyles are not only used for drainage, but are also important decorative ornamentation on the terrace.

Works, and Ruan An, a eunuch in the Ming Court. In fact, the person who contributed most to the planning and design was Cai Xin, who had learned craftsmanship since his childhood, experienced different trades of construction works and later became a skillful planner and designer. His works were respected by the master craftsmen of different trades.

Xu Gao was a carpenter. In 1557 (36th year of Ming Emperor Jiajing), the Three Great Halls, the Literary Building (later Pavilion of Manifest Benevolence), the Military Building (later Pavilion of Glorifying Righteousness) and neighboring buildings were all destroyed by lightning fire. As those halls and buildings had been built over a hundred years, no detailed design drawings were left. Depending on the investigation of the ruins and the recall of the destroyed buildings, Xu Gao and his colleague Lei Li carried out a restoration design. Five years later, the buildings were all restored, and it was generally acknowledged that they were nearly the same as the originals. Due to a shortage of sized timber logs, Xu Gao created a new type of column, each built up of several small timbers fastened with wrought iron stirrup straps. His creation had saved on a great deal of construction funds, namely, "It was estimated over million taels, but it turned out to be only one tenth of it". Later he was also promoted to an official of the Board of Works.

Liang Jiu, a carpenter in the early Qing Dynasty, was born in Shuntian Prefecture (now Beijing). He was a disciple of Feng Qiao, a famous master carpenter in the late Ming Dynasty. From Feng, he learned how to make scale models. In 1695 (34th year of Emperor Kangxi), Liang Jiu took charge of the reconstruction of the Hall of Supreme Harmony, destroyed by fire 16 years before. He made a model of the Hall of Supreme Harmony with a scale of 1 to 10 for the emperor to approve as well as for supervising the site work. The existing Hall of Supreme Harmony was designed by Liang Jiu.

Lei Fada, designer and modeler of the first generation of the "Modeler Lei Family", came to Beijing to serve the Court in the early years of the reign period of Emperor Kangxi. While designing a building or a building complex, he made drawings in definite scale and cardboard models. The roof of the building models might be removed to show its interior decorations. Models of such kind are called "waxed models" for the last procedure of making them was polishing with melted wax. The craft of Modeler Lei Family was handed down through seven generations until the end of the Qing Dynasty, spanning a period of more than 240 years. Part of Modeler Lei Family's models and drawings are now preserved in the Forbidden City.

# The Imperial Palace in Shenyang

## —— A Jewel of Manchu, Han, Mongolian, and Tibetan Architecture

The Imperial Palace in Shenyang is a magnificent architectural complex built during the Qing Dynasty. Although much less in grandeur and scale than the Imperial Palace in Beijing, it is the best example of Manchu architecture in China. Shenyang was where the Manchus rose and prospered. The Manchu rulers, both before and after they crossed the Great Wall and entered northern China, had the palace renovated and expanded continually. Built in a unique style, the palace is now the only object of study for scholars interested in early Qing Dynasty construction.

**The Dazheng Hall**

Located at the northern end of the central axis of the East Section, the hall is the earliest palatial building constructed in the Imperial Palace in Shenyang. Facing south, it has an octagonal plan and pyramidal roof with double tiers of eaves. The roof is covered with yellow glazed titles and edged with green ones. The two vermillion columns directly in front of the hall are each decorated with a golden dragon. The hall is characteristic of buildings constructed before the Qing Dynasty crossed the Great Wall and entered North China.

The Chongzheng Hall

Located in the front courtyard of the Middle Section, the hall was rebuilt in 1762, the 27th year under the reign of Emperor Qianlong. Although it is an important work of architecture on the central axis of the Middle Section, it has only a simple gabled roof without overhangs, showing that a more matured form of Han palatial architecture was yet to be adopted.

## I. General Layout of the Imperial Palace

Judging from architectural concepts, Chinese palace architecture was closely related to the Chinese ideology of the land and agriculture and the worship of heaven and ancestors. Palace buildings were erected around a courtyard, closed to the outside world. The individual buildings comprising a palace complex differed from each other in form and size according to the seniority of the respective users and their positions in the feudal hierarchy. The layout of the Imperial Palace in Shenyang, like that of the Imperial Palace in Beijing, shows a strong influence of ancient China's system of hierarchy and ethics.

The Imperial Palace in Shenyang can be divided into three sections-east, middle and west. The East Section contains the Dazheng Hall and Ten-Prince Pavilions built by Nurhachi and the Middle Section contains the imperial residence built by his son and successor, Huangtaiji. In the West Section are the Jiayin Hall, the Pavilion of Literary Reminiscence, the Yangxi Study, and the theater, built by Emperor Qianlong. He also added two groups of buildings,

**Decorated Gable of the Pavilion of Respecting Ancestors**

Located in the East Lodge of the Middle Section, the pavilion was built during Emperor Qianlong's time. Gables of the gable-and-hipped roofs of important imperial buildings are often decorated – another characteristic of resplendent royal buildings.

known as the East and West Lodges, in the east and west sides of the Middle Section for his use when he visited the secondary capital. The site of the Imperial Palace is rectangular, the longer sides running east and west and shorter one running north and south. The entire palace covers an area of 63,272.53 $m^2$ and consists of 96 buildings with 419 jian, or rooms, totaling 16,421.34 $m^2$ in floor space.

### 1. Imperial Palace with Distinct Axes and Clear Functional Areas

There is a north-south axis in each of the three Sections of the palace complex and two secondary north-south axes that run through the East and West Lodges in the Middle Section. Although the three sections were built in different periods of time and separated by walls, they were so well designed that they blended with each other harmoniously and form a coherent whole. Both the main and lesser buildings in the palace complex are tastefully arranged, clearly showing the ranks and social status of their users.

**Back View of the Phoenix Tower**

Located to the north of the Chongzheng Hall, the tower was rebuilt in 1762. The Phoenix Tower and five other palaces – Palace of Purity and Tranquility, Guanju Palace, Yanqing Palace, Linzhi Palace, and Yongfu Palace – are built on a high terrace 3.8 m high. In the Imperial Palace in Shenyang, palaces are built on high terrace, and halls are built on level ground.

The main structure on the axis in the East Section is the Dazheng Hall where Nurhachi held court. On the right and left sides of the axis are the Ten-Prince Pavilions, arranged in the shape of the Chinese character "八". The pavilions were the offices of the Prince of the Right Wing, the Prince of the Left Wing, and the heads of the Eight Banners. (The Eight Banners were the flags of the eight divisions of Nurhachi's troops, each flag having its own colour. Nurhachi appointed his sons and nephews as heads of the eight divisions). Built in perfect proportion and tastefully decorated, they blend well with each other.

The Middle Section consists of the front and back parts, known as the outer and inner courts respectively. The main building on the axis in the middle of the outer court is the Chongzheng Hall where the emperor conducted the administration of the empire. Opposite the hall toward the south is the Gate of Great Qing where civil and military officials would wait every morning for the emperor to appear in court. The inner court, or the residential quarters of the imperial family, has five palaces. The main palace was the empress' chamber which stands on the axis. Arranged in symmetry on both sides of the axis are four lesser palaces which served as the chambers of the emperor's secondary wives. The five palaces in the inner court are so built and arranged that their locations and sizes strictly conformed to the order of seniority of the users and their positions in the feudal hierarchy. The East and West Lodges which served as living quarters for the emperor when he made an inspection tour of the secondary capital are also built in accordance with the social status and the order of seniority of the users.

Standing on the axis between the Chongzheng Hall and the Palace of Purity and Tranquillity is the magnificent Phoenix Tower, built on a high terrace. The tower greatly enhances the change of space in the Middle Section and the visual beauty of its buildings as a whole. If the group of palatial buildings in the Middle Section is compared to a measure of beautiful music, the tower is one of its most sweet-sounding notes. Structures like the Phoenix Tower can also be found on the secondary axes in the Middle Section, all gracefully arranged and blending well with their surroundings.

The group of buildings along the axis in the West Section were used as studies, lounges, and recreation rooms by the emperor when he visited Shenyang. The buildings in this section are likewise erected in accordance with rigid seniority standards. For example, the Jiayin Hall which stands directly right on the axis is a throne room where the emperor looked out and watched operas.

**Entrance to the West Lodge**

On the east and west sides of the middle section are the East Lodge (the Yihe Hall, the Jiezhi Palace, and the Pavilion of Respecting Classics) and the West lodge (the Diguang Hall, the Palace of Preserving Supremacy, the Jisi Study, and the Chongmo Pavilion). These two complexes were added during Emperor Qianlong's time.

**Apron of the Theatrical Stage**

Located in the front courtyard of the Jiayin Hall in the West Section, the stage was built in 1782, the 47th year under the reign of Emperor Qianlong. It is open on three sides and sits on a raised platform 90 cm high. The ceiling has an octagonal caisson with a sitting dragon in the centre, The coffered ceiling around it is decorated with crane patterns.

**Two Columns with Coiling Dragons in front of the Dazheng Hall**

The dragons, circling three times around the columns, have heads stretched out from the columns to reach for a flaming pearl between them. One of their front claws rest on the lintel, the other is stretched behind them. Their hind claws and tails grip the columns tightly.

On either side of the axis are galleries from which his ministers could enjoy the performances. The palace building, being the embodiment of royal power, were always designed in such a way that imperial supremacy and dignity had the clearest manifestation possible.

### 2. The Arrangement of Courtyards in the Imperial Palace

The Imperial Palace in Shenyang has a number of courtyards enclosed either by buildings, by walls or by corridors. Different in form and size, they greatly enrich the variation of space in the palace complex.

The courtyard in front of the Dazheng Hall in the East Section is flanked by the Ten Prince Pavilions on both sides with a long, straight path for the use

**Gable Springer of the Gate of Great Qing** / left

Specific glazed titles with dragon patterns decorate the springers of gable walls on both sides of the gate, some with their heads upward, others downward – all looking lively and active.

**Skirt Panel of a Partition Door in the Dazheng Hall** / right

The Dazheng Hall is octagonal in plan with a double-eaved pyramidal roof. Each of its eight elevation surfaces has a suite of partition doors installed. The skirt panels of the partition doors are decorated with dragons coiled in round frames. The two dragons on the two adjacent door panels face each other.

of the emperor through the middle.

The courtyard in front of the Chongzheng Hall is square in plan, spacious and surrounded by buildings on all sides. The courtyard, combined with flights of steps known as the imperial way leading up to a terrace in front of the splendid hall, the long stone ramp carved with dragons in the centre of the central flight, and the sundial and the grain measure on the terrace, sets off the hall and makes it even move awe-inspiring. The courtyard behind the Phoenix Tower is enclosed by residential palaces built on a high terrace, giving visitors a feeling of harmony and cheerfulness.

The courtyards in the West Section vary in shape. The Garden of Herbaceous Peony is a courtyard enclosed by a corridor connecting the Pavilion of Literary Reminiscence and the Yangxi Study. The courtyard between the Jiayin Hall and the theater is flanked by galleries and sealed off from the outside

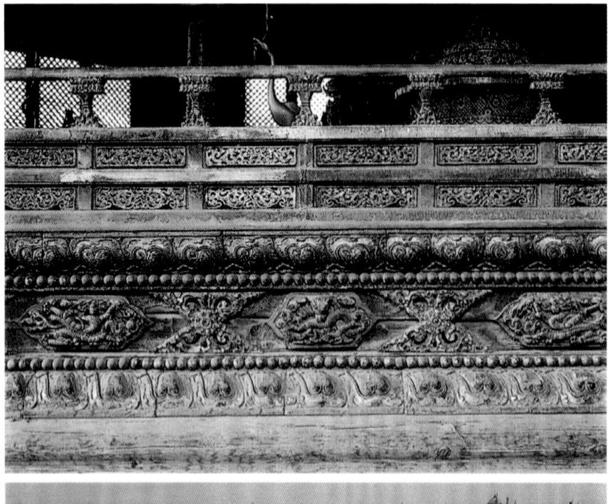

**The Sumeru Dais in the Dazheng Hall**

This interior Sumeru dais is decorated with conches on the top and dragon designs in the middle. This is one of wood while most Sumeru bases in traditional Chinese architecture are of stone or brick.

**Panoramic View of the Dazheng Hall and the Ten-Prince Pavilions**

The Ten-Prince Pavilions flank both sides of the Dazheng Hall – five to the east and five to the west. The two nearest to the hall are the Pavilions of the Left Wing Prince and the Right Wing Prince respectively. The other eight pavilions are arranged in a swallow-tail fashion according to the order of the Eight Banners.

by high walls on two sides. This not only helps enhance the acoustics of the theater but, also provides a pleasing environment for the audience to enjoy the performances.

### 3. The High-Terrace Architecture

High-terrace architecture was developed by the Nuzhen people when they inhabited high mountain slopes. The five residential palaces and the Phoenix Tower in the Middle Section built by Huangtaiji are erected on a terrace 3.8 m high. The throne hall built on the ground to the south of the residential palaces is much lower. This is just the opposite of the elevation design of the Imperial Palace in Beijing. The five residential palaces and the Phoenix Tower are enclosed by a 2.5 m high inner wall with an outer wall one metre higher than the inner one, forming a square castle sealed off from the outside. In between the two walls is a narrow path 90 cm wide for night patrol.

## II. Design of Individual Palatial Buildings

Palatial buildings constructed in Shenyang before the Manchus crossed the Great Wall in 1644 show the influence of the architecture of the Song and Yuan dynasties. Their brackets sets are not compact and are painted in warm colours. In 1734, the 12th year of the Yongzheng reign, the Qing court promulgated the Construction Regulations drawn up by the Ministry of Works of the Qing Dynasty. The buildings in the East and West Lodges and the West Section, erected between the 11th and 48th years of the reign of Qianlong, were constructed in accordance with the regulations. Compared with the early

**An Imperial Throne in the Chongzheng Hall**

Located in the front courtyard of the Middle Section, the Hall was the place where Huangtaiji handled government affairs. A throne with an openwork dragon design as well as a gilded lacquered screen are placed on a dais. In front are two columns decorated with flying dragons.

buildings in the palace complex, they are more elegant, splendid, and stylized and are a reflection of the political life, religious customs, and architectural aesthetics of the Qing Dynasty.

### 1. Dazheng Hall

Located at the northern end of the axis of the east section, the Dazheng Hall is the earliest palatial building constructed in the Imperial Palace in Shenyang. Here the emperor ascended the throne and held grand ceremonies. Modelled after the Octagonal Hall in Liaoyang, it stands on an eight-sided Sumeru platform 1.5 m high with each side measuring nine m long. A long, straight imperial way leads up to the hall from the south. There is a verandah around the hall with stone balustrades carved with lotus leaves and Buddhist vessels on the outer sides of the platform. The hall has a pyramidal roof with double tiers of eaves. The roof is covered with yellow glazed tiles and edged with green ones. The bracket sets under the eaves are of double tiers projected

**Glazed Ceramic Decorations on the Gables of the Chongzheng Hall**

The slanting ridges and the verge boards on the top of the gable walls of the Hall are decorated with blue glazed dragons, one following the other, running upwards. The dragons themselves and the reddish brownflame and dark blue pearl in front of each dragon are set off by designs of green water and colourful clouds. This picture of dragons chasing pearls gives the gables a highly ornamental verge.

**A Caisson with a Descending Dragon in the Dazheng Hall**

The top layer of the caisson has a golden carved descending dragon in the centre. The intermediate layer is surrounded by eight trapezoid coffers decorated with round lotus petals. Each lotus petal has a different Sanskrit character which strongly suggests the Lamaism of the Qing Dynasty.

with double ang. The peristyle and hypostyle columns in the hall are all round. Two peristyle columns of the central bay in front of the hall are each decorated with a golden dragon coiling upward. The coffered ceiling with a caisson is splendidly painted with a descending dragon in the centre of the caisson and Chinese and Sanskrit words on the ceiling boards.

The paved imperial way is flanked by the Ten-Prince Pavilions. The pavilions, square in shape and equal in size, have brick walls on three sides, and the front sides are made up of latticed wooden partitions with door leaves. They each have a verandah around them. The columns that support the eaves are square except those at the corners, which are round. They are crowned with gable-and hipped roofs covered with grey tiles. The buildings are arranged in

**The Throne in the Dazheng Hall**

The back and the armrests of the imperial throne are carved with openwork dragon designs. The dragons, with their heads raised and their scales carved meticulously, are in a lively posture, ready to soar into the sky. The yellow silk cushion on the throne highlights the supreme power of the emperor.

the shape of the Chinese character for "eight" (八) symbolizing the political and military system of the Eight Banners introduced by Nurhachi.

### 2. Chongzheng Hall

Completed at the same time as the Gate of Great Qing, the hall was where Huangtaiji held court, received high officials, and celebrated important festivals. Similar to the Gate of Great Qing in architectural form and style, it is a five-bay hall capped with a gabled roof and has a verandah in front and in back. The main ridge and four side ridges are embellished with colour-glazed decorations. In front of the hall are stone balustrades with flights of steps in the central part leading up to the hall. In the centre of the central flight is a long stone ramp carved with a design of two dragons playing with a ball. The peristyle

**The Animal-faced Decoration of the Chongzheng Hall**

Besides adopting traditional Han techniques, the Imperial Palace in Shenyang also assimilates Lamaist architecture in decorations. The wooden decoration above the upper end of the column manifests this religious influence. The animal head in the centre has the face of a lion and the horns of a goat. It is decorated on both sides with scroll designs.

**Decorative Paintings on the Roof Beams in the Chongzheng Hall**

The Chongzheng Hall has no ceiling apart from the interior of the roof itself. The exposed beams of the roof are decorated with hexi paintings rich in colours characteristic of the region. In some of the paintings, the central part of the beam is painted with baofu (wrapper) like the Su-style paintings. In these baofu paintings, golden dragons are painted on a background of red while powder paste is trickled on raised lines. There are also blue clouds and flaming pearls

columns are square and the hypostyle columns, round. Doors and windows are all exquisitely latticed. In the centre of the hall is a T-shaped dais on which the throne stands with a golden lacquer screen behind it. The throne is gilded and carved in a dragon pattern. Arranged on the east and west sides of the terrace in front of the hall are a sundial and a grain measure. The construction of entrance doorframe of the hall is similar to those of the Ten Prince Pavilions.

### 3. Phoenix Tower

The tower, topped with gable-and-hipped roof, is the only palatial building using the bracket system constructed by Huangtaiji. In this building, the emperor often invited his ministers to dinner and discussed politics with them. He also used it as a resting place. After the Manchus made Beijing their capital, the tower was used for housing historical relics such as the portraits of the Qing rulers of all previous generations. Square in plan, it has three bays in width and depth, and seven purlins from front to back with verandahs on the four sides. The door on the ground floor opens into the courtyard enclosed by the residential palaces built on a high terrace. The second story of the tower has a coffered ceiling with a caisson in the centre decorated with Chinese and Sanskrit words and phoenix patterns. The beams and brackets of the three-storied tower are all beautifully patterned against a red background, and the roof is covered with yellow glazed tiles and edged with green ones. As the tallest building in Shenyang at that time, it was the best place for watching the sunrise in the city and was known as one of Shenyang's "Eight Scenes". The tower is similar

in forms and styles to those built in the lower and middle reaches of the Yellow River in China.

### 4. Palace of Purity and Tranquillity

Located at the northern end of the central axis of the Middle Section, this palace was where Huangtaiji, known as Emperor Taizong of the Qing Dynasty, and his empress lived. On its east and west sides are the four lesser palaces which housed Huangtaiji's concubines -- Chen, Gui, Shu, and Zhuang. These buildings form a square compound along with the Phoenix Tower. The Palace of Purity and Tranquillity has five bays in width and eleven purlins from front to back with verandahs in front and in back. It has a gabled roof covered with

**Decorative Paintings on the Beams of the Palace of Purity and Tranquility**
opposite page

In the central part of the beams, painted with baodu patterns, a curved line encircles two gilded dragons with powder paste trickled on raised lines amid blue clouds and flaming pearls. The round pictures on the coffered ceiling have a dragon and phoenix set off by blue and green. They are in striking contrast to the warm vermillion of the beams.

**Chimney Behind the Palace of Purity and Tranquility**

The chimney, erected two m to the west behind the palace, is one of the characteristics of the life of the Manchus reflected in heating devices. There are similar chimneys behind the Palace of Earthly Tranquility and Palace of Tranquil Longevity in the Forbidden City in Beijing.

**Stove Opening Outside the East Warm Chamber of the Palace of Purity and Tranquility**

The chamber has two heatable brick bed, one on the southern side and the other on the northern side. Outside the window is a triangular stove opening constructed with eight layers of bricks. Below is a square stokehole.

**An Interior View of the Pavilion of Literary Reminiscence** / opposite page

An imperial throne is placed in the central bay of the Pavilion of Literary Reminiscence. In front of the throne there is a carved desk holding writing brushes, ink slabs, ink sticks and paper. Behind the throne is a screen.

yellow glazed tiles and edged with green ones. The roof ridges are decorated with dragon and phoenix motifs.

The palace is built in the Manchu style, with the entrance not in the middle but far toward the eastern side. The east end bay of the palace is called the Eastern Warm Chamber. A perforate partition screen divides the chamber into a north and a south room. The chamber served as Huangtaiji's bedroom. It has a heatable brick bed in the south room and an ordinary bed in the north room. Next to the chamber on the west is a spacious room with four bays in width. It was used for worshipping Shamanist gods and spirits. Along the east, west and north walls are brick beds decorated with symbols of good fortune and longevity.

**5. Pavilion of Literary Reminiscence**

Built in 1781, the 46th year of Emperor Qianlong's reign, and modelled after the famous Tianyige Pavilion in Ningbo, it is one of the seven buildings designed as a book repository to store *the "Complete Collection in Four Treasures"* (Si Ku Quan Shu), a huge encyclopedic collection of ancient and contemporary works compiled between 1773 and 1781. The pavilion has six bays in width and nine purlins from front to back with covered verandahs in front and at the back.

The west end bay is about two m in width with a staircase leading to the upper floor of the building. It appears to have two stories from the outside but actually has a mezzanine floor between the two. The mezzanine floor is unpartitioned with an overhang corridor two m in depth on the north side. The pavilion is painted mostly in cold colours and covered with a gabled roof with double eaves. The roof is covered with black glazed tiles and edged with green ones and its ridges are decorated with patterns of clouds and waves.

The Excellence of Ancient Chinese Architecture

# Palace Architecture

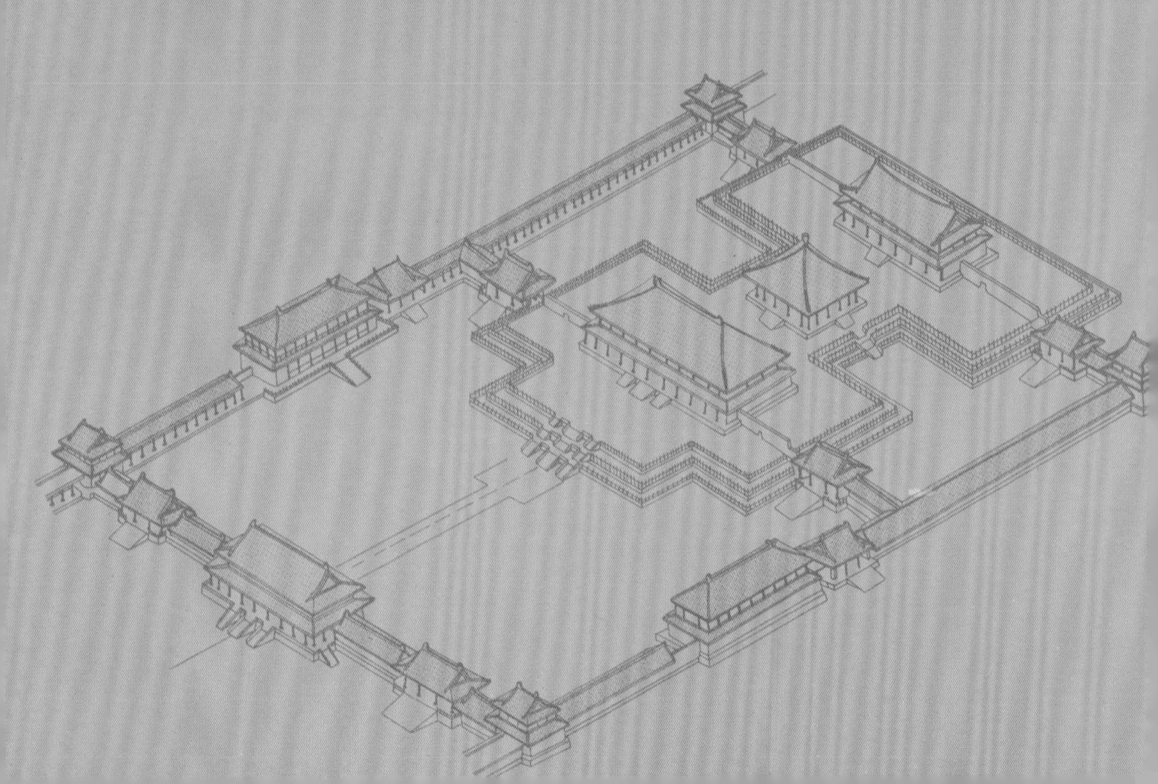

# Notes on the Photographs

## Imperial Palaces of the Last Dynasty

### The Forbidden City in Beijing

The Forbidden City in Beijing was first built in 1406 AD, the fourth year of the reign of Yongle, which was the title of Emperor Zhudi of the Ming Dynasty. The Forbidden City consists of two parts: the Outer Court in the south, the Inner Court in the north. All principal buildings are laid out on its central axis from south to north. The Three Great Halls on a high axial terrace are the main halls of the Outer Court. The Hall of Supreme Harmony is the most typical and representative building of the three. The Palace of Heavenly Purity is the main building among the palaces in the Inner Court. Behind these palaces, there is the Imperial Garden which used to be a recreation place for the emperors. To the east and west of the Palace of Heavenly Purity, there are the East Six Palaces and the West Six Palaces of the Inner Court. Each palace has its own axis parallel to the central one. All these building complexes constitute a huge integrated architectural complex enclosed by city walls. The city walls with a wide moat around were not only the protective works, they also formed a closed life style for the imperial family, apart from the outside world and unknown by the common people. People could not enter into the City to see what it looked like and to know what the royal life used to be until the disintegration of the feudal dynasty. In this book, the colour pictures of the Forbidden City are to show you its splendid panorama, and then, to guide you passing through its front entrance, the Meridian Gate, along the central axis from the Outer Court to the Inner in order to reveal the mystery of the imperial city of the last feudal dynasty.

### The Imperial Palace in Shenyang

The Imperial Palace in Shenyang was built during the reign of the Manchu Emperor Nurhachi, Shenzu of the Qing Dynasty. It had been the political centre until 1644 when the Manchus rushed into Beijing and seized the dominant position to rule over the whole country. The Imperial Palace in Shenyang consists of three building complexes: the Middle, the East and West. Each has its own political function and architectural style, as well as its own south-north central axis. The Middle Section is the largest of the three. It has two subsidiary complexes, or lodges, attached to its east and west for the emperor and empress to stay in temporarily when they were out on inspection tours. The Chongzheng Hall, and the Pavilion of Phoenix and the Palace of Purity and Tranquility are the main structures of the Middle Section, where the Manchu emperor Huangtaiji used to live and conduct the state affairs. The architectural style of these buildings is a combination of styles of several nationalities. The Dazheng Hall is the main building located on the northern end of the axis of the East Section. In front of it, there are ten pavilions called the Ten-Prince Pavilions, which indicate the features of the regime in the early Qing period. The regime was based and focused on Manchurian military-administrative organization, the Eight Banners. The West Section used to be the place for recreation and for keeping books and scriptures. A library called Pavilion of Literary Reminiscence was the main building in the West Section.

## The Forbidden City Viewed from the Prospect Hill

The Forbidden City, which served as the imperial palace during the Ming and Qing dynasties, was built in 1406. The layout remains roughly the same despite the fact that most existing buildings were erected during the Qing Dynasty. The two main categories of major buildings—imperial palaces in the front and residential

quarters in the rear—are arranged along a south-north axis, with ancillary buildings laid out symmetrically on either side. The general layout features a clear demarcation between major and minor buildings, with space impeccably partitioned and grouped, and emphasis placed on a few landmark structures. The massive and splendid Forbidden City is the largest and best preserved palatial group in China.

### The Imperial Way to the Gate of Supreme Harmony and the Hall of Supreme Harmony

The Gate of Supreme Harmony was given its present name during the early Qing Dynasty. The gate was built in the 18th year in the Yongle reign of Ming Emperor Chengzu and was rebuilt during the Guangxu reign of Qing Emperor Dezong. The gate, which is nine bays wide and sits on an elevated marble terrace, features front and rear access to the imperial way. The Gate of Supreme Harmony has a gable-and-hipped roof with double eaves and is the tallest structure of its kind in the Forbidden City. The gate towers over an extensive courtyard and faces the Meridian Gate to the south. Five white marble bridges span the Inner Golden River flowing in front of the structure, with the expansive rear courtyard highlighting the supreme position of the Hall of Supreme Harmony in the distance. This photo captures a glimpse of the imperial way stretching north of the Gate of Supreme Harmony. (Photo by Hu Chui)

**General Plan of the Three Great Halls Complex, the Outer Court**

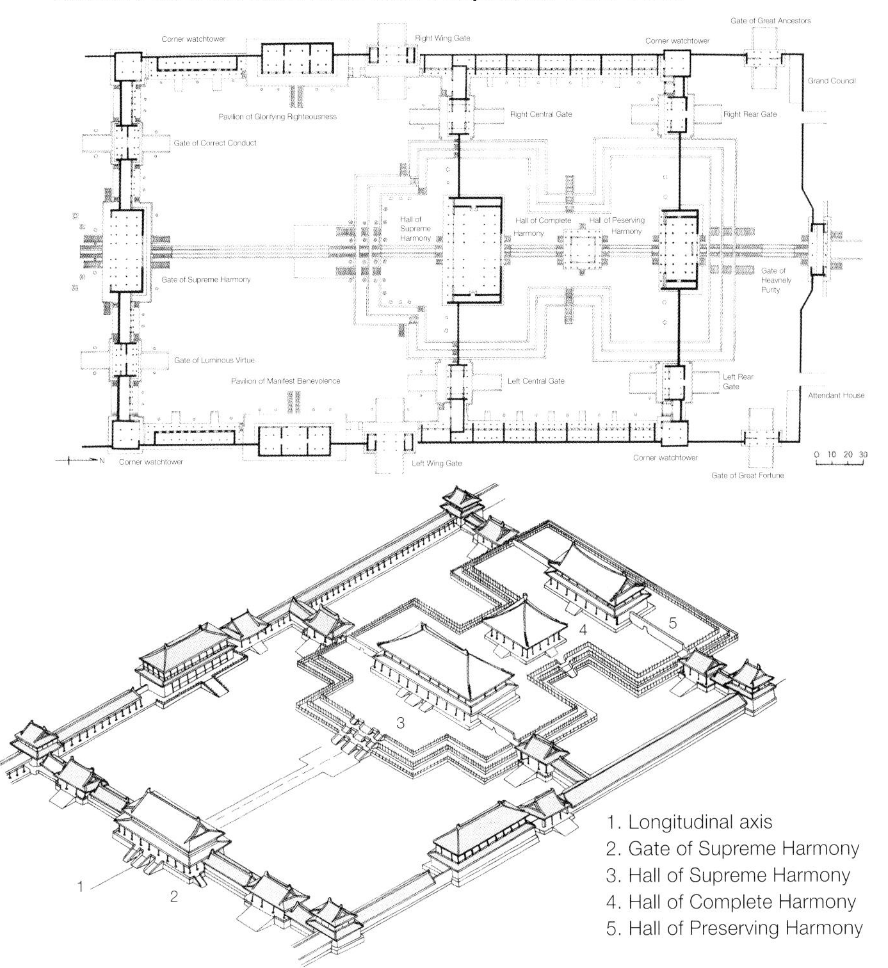


**Diagram of the Three Great Halls Complex, the Outer Court**

The magnificent Gate of Supreme Harmony in the outer court opens to the three great halls—the Hall of Supreme Harmony, Hall of Complete Harmony and Hall of Preserving Harmony. The three great halls are the focus of the Outer Court and the culmination of the central axis in the Forbidden City.

The three great halls combine the principles of traditional layouts of courts. The small Hall of Complete Harmony (a square pavilion) sits between the larger Hall of Supreme Harmony (front) and Hall of Preserving Harmony (rear). The arrangement, which alleviates the monotony of two huge rectangular halls and sets off large against small, creates a brilliant space effect with differences between main and secondary buildings and a rhythmic sense of rising and falling outlines.

## General Plan of the Forbidden City in Beijing

The Forbidden City, in the centre of Beijing, occupies an area of 720 000 $m^2$. and has total floor space of some 150 000 $m^2$. The orderly and integrated arrangement of palace halls with more than 9000 rooms, present a splendid air. The Forbidden City is the world's most magnificent and best-preserved palace complex.

A large number of buildings are arranged along the central axis in the Forbidden City, from the Gate of Great Qing to the Prospect Hill. Main buildings are placed precisely along the axis line and auxiliary buildings arranged in symmetric layouts. The layout creates a neat and majestic atmosphere and forms a unified architectural style.

The main buildings in the Forbidden City are arranged in conformity with *the Survey on Construction Work* collected in *the Ritual of Zhou*, as well as the traditional rites of Chinese feudal society, e.g. the Imperial Ancestral Temple is located to the front left of the Forbidden City, with the Altar of Land and Grain sitting on the front right; three great halls and five gates are found in the outer court on the central axis, with three rear palaces in the inner court.

1. Gate of Great Qing
2. Gate of Heavenly Peace (Tian An Men)
3. Gate of Correct Demeanor
4. Altar of Land and Grain
5. Imperial Ancestral Temple
6. Meridian Gate
7. West Glorious Gate
8. Hall of Military Eminence
9. Gate of Supreme Harmony
10. Hall of Literary Glory
11. East Glorious Gate
12. Hall of Supreme Harmony
13. Palace of Heavenly Purity
14. Gate of Heavenly Purity
15. Imperial Garden
16. Gate of Divine Might
17. Prospect Hill
18. Memorial Hall of Late Emperors

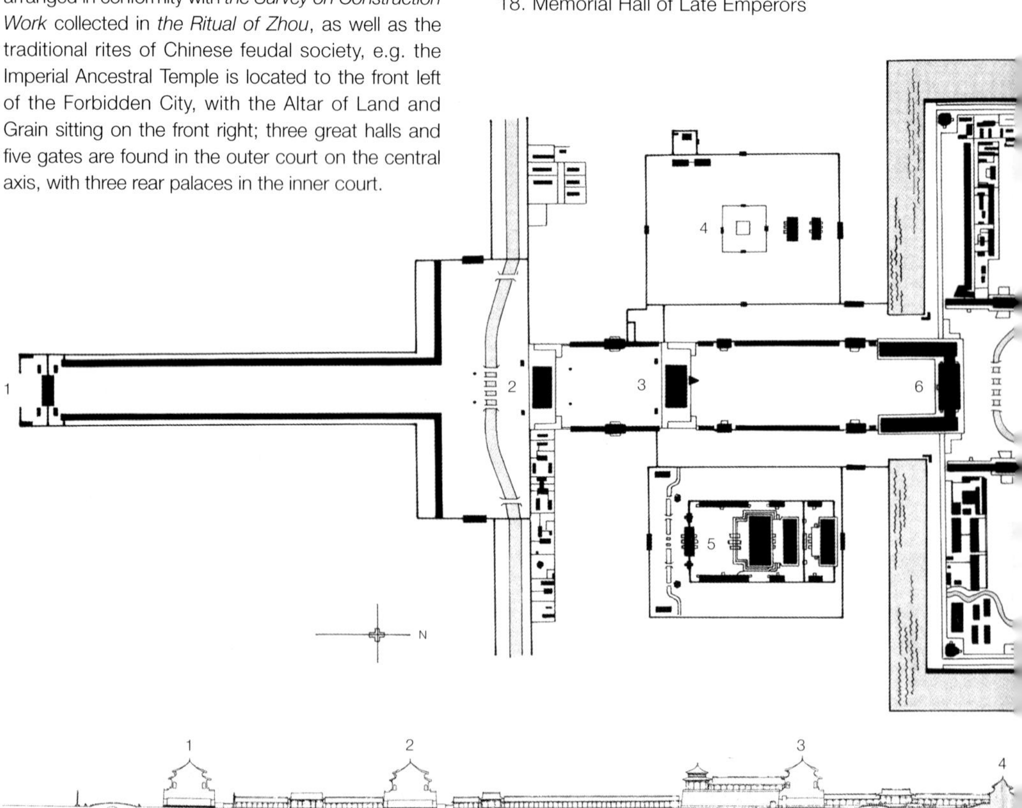

## Longitudinal Section of the Forbidden City, Beijing

The layout of the buildings along the central axis of the Forbidden City, from the main gate of the Imperial City to the Gate of Divine Might and the North Grand Gate, provides a general view at the master plan of the Forbidden City.

This sectional drawing shows the integration of the main and secondary buildings, altered spaces, sequence of layouts and variations of rising and falling outlines. The three great halls stand on a three-tiered white marble terrace.

1. Gate of Heavenly Peace
2. Gate of Correct Demeanor
3. Meridian Gate
4. Gate of Supreme Harmony
5. Pavilion of Manifest Benevolence
6. Hall of Supreme Harmony
7. Hall of complete Harmony
8. Hall of Preserving Harmony
9. Gate of Heavenly Purity
10. Palace of Heavenly Purity
11. Hall of Union
12. Palace of Earthly Tranquility
13. Gate of Earthly Tranquility
14. Hall of Imperial Peace
15. Gate of Divine Might
16. North Grand Gate

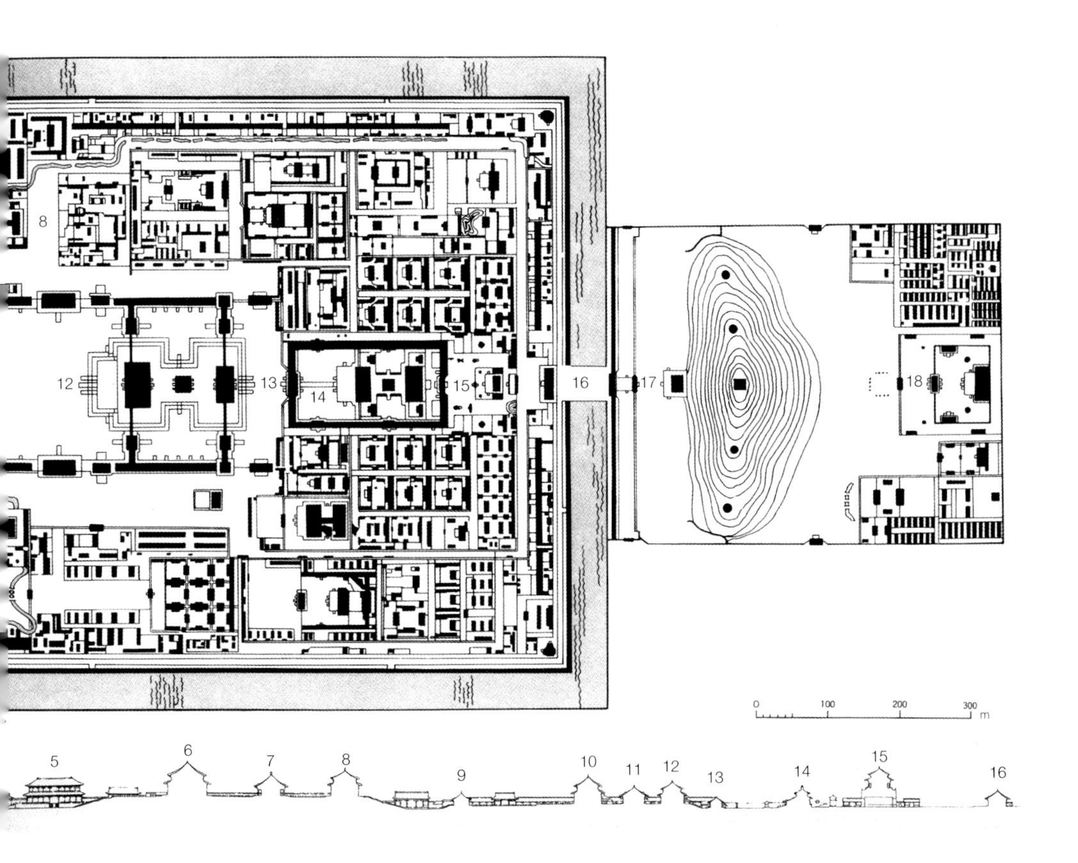

## Meridian Gate from the Perspective of the Inner Golden River

Entering the Forbidden City through the Meridian Gate provides one with a magnificent view of five exquisitely crafted marble bridges spanning the inner golden river as it threads its way across the compound and disappears behind the palace walls. The banks of the river are lined with marble balustrades whose crudely carved gourd-shaped capitals highlight the pomp and pageantry associated with the Meridian Gate. The gate, skirted by vermillion walls on three sides and flanked by corner pavilions, rises above the river and soars into the azure heavens evoking the awesome atmosphere of imperial days. Marble balustrades lining the inner golden river as it follows an eastern track across the compound are suggestive of a jade belt winding its way beneath a blue sky dotted with white clouds. The resulting imagery mitigates some of the harshness of the Meridian Gate and adds a graceful air to the entire scene.

## The Pavilion of Manifest Benevolence

The existing structure was rebuilt during the Qianlong reign of the Qing Dynasty. The pavilion, which is elevated on a high terrace, is nine bays wide and three bays deep, and features a hipped roof covered with yellow glazed tiles. The pavilion, which from the outside appears to be a two story structure, actually has three interior floors. Three layers of bracket sets grace the upper eaves, mezzanine and lower eaves respectively. Beams and lintels are decorated with lower rank xuanzi decorative paintings highlighted by a single-stroke fang xin in the centre. The structure forms a symmetrical pattern flanking the Hall of Supreme Harmony and the Pavilion of Enhanced Righteousness. The Pavilion of Manifest Benevolence played an indispensable role in ancient times serving as the site of the treasury and a warehouse for garments, silk and leather goods, as well as a supply station for porcelain tea sets.

## The Inner Golden River / upper

The inner golden river comes from the west as it flows through the Forbidden City, and eventually disappears beyond the walls. Ancient Chinese believed the five elements-metal, wood, water, fire and earth-formed the physical universe, and the west, where the river comes from, corresponds to metal, including gold. Hence the name, Golden River. The multifunctional river is divided into two sections, with the outer golden river flowing in front of the Gate of Heavenly Peace, and the inner golden river meandering across the better half of the Forbidden City before exiting the southeast corner of the compound and emptying into the moat. The river is the main source of water for the Forbidden City, with surface runoff channeled through a drainage network running north, south, east and west into the inner golden river. The photo offers a glimpse of the Tower of Loftiness, the gable-and-hipped roof structure, to the left of the Gate of Supreme Harmony.

## Corner Pavilion of the Meridian Gate and the Moat / lower

The steeply-banked surrounding moat was not only befitting of the Forbidden City's function as the imperial palace, but also provided protection for the emperor and his court. In sharp contrast, the Meridian Gate features a U-shaped plan, and is flanked on either side by a thirteen-bay gallery and two corner pavilions. The towering central gate and four corner pavilions resemble five peaks, hence the nickname—Five-Phoenix Towers. Corner pavilions are each square in plan, with a double-eaved pyramidal roof topped with a gilded bronze roof pommel. While the view of the Meridian Gate from the banks of the moat is partially blocked, reflections of the gallery and corner pavilions can be seen quivering in the limpid water on a bright sunny day. The reflected silhouettes not only add to the serenity of the Meridian Gate and the mystery of the Forbidden City, but also inspire a feeling of nostalgia in the hearts of beholders.

## Bronze Lion (upper) Guarding the Gate of Supreme Harmony

Pairs of stone or bronze lions, ferocious beasts known as the "king of animals", often guarded the front gates of palaces, temples, imperial tombs and other major buildings in ancient China. Bronze lions in the Forbidden City can be found in front of the Gate of Supreme Harmony, Gate of Heavenly Purity, Gate of Mental Cultivation, Gate of Eternal Spring, Gate of Tranquil Longevity, and Gate of Spiritual Cultivation. The largest pair of bronze lions sits in front of the Gate of Supreme Harmony. The gate, the largest of its kind which serves as the entrance to the three great halls in the outer court, is adorned with the highest class ornamentation found in the Forbidden City. The bronze lions, which crouch on bronze pedestals with Sumeru bases, highlight the awe-inspiring dimensions of the Gate of Supreme Harmony.

## Bronze Lion (lower) Guarding the Gate of Supreme Harmony

As mentioned before, sculptured lions often flanked the gates of major buildings in ancient China. A lioness with a lionet playing under her left front paw guarded the right flank, while a heroic male lion with his right front paw resting on a ball sat to the left.  Photos here illustrate the pair of lions guarding the Gate of Supreme Harmony. The lioness in the lower photo, a paragon of maternal love, inspires awe which lacks any trace of grotesqueness. The male lion (upper) strikes a courageous pose with one paw resting on a ball. A finely crafted bronze bell hanging down from its neck bears the image of an fierce lion. Despite the ravages of time and the elements, the sharpness of sculpted detail on this rare piece of Chinese bronze sculpture remain untarnished.

## Stone Carving on the Imperial Ramp Fronting the Hall of Supreme Harmony

The imperial ramp, famous for its ornately carved flagstones, was set in the central part of the Imperial Way flanked by flights of steps for the exclusive use of the emperor, who on special occasions entered and departed the hall in a sedan chair borne by porters. No one in China, from the wealthiest man in the country to the most powerful dukes, generals and ministers, was permitted to build a ramp equaling the grandeur of the Imperial Way or Royal Path. Stone slabs on the ramp were chiselled with likenesses of dragons in lively postures. The Imperial Ramp leading to the Hall of Supreme Harmony, which is 16.57 m long and 3.07 m wide, consists of three huge stone slabs carved with nine serpentine dragons frolicking in the clouds. Joints between the slabs were cleverly camouflaged with cloud-like tracery.

## Facade of the Hall of Supreme Harmony

The Hall of Supreme Harmony, the most prestigious of the three great halls in the outer court, is the foremost architectural structure in the Forbidden City. The hall is 11 bays (60.01 m) wide and five bays (33.33 m) deep. The Hall of Supreme Harmony has 55 jian or rooms, with the space between every four columns countered as a jian, or a single room. The structure, which has a hipped roof and double eaves, stands 37.44 m in height and sits on a terrace covering 2,377 $m^2$. The photo shows the immenseness of the Hall of Supreme Harmony from the perspective of the Gate of Supreme Harmony. The expansive courtyard between the gate and the hall symbolized the omnipetence of imperial authority. At the bottom of the photo are the carved flagstones of the Imperial Ramp of the Gate of Supreme Harmony.

## Front Elevation, Section and Plan of the Hall of Supreme Harmony

The Hall of Supreme Harmony, also known as the Hall of Golden Chimes, served as the main venue for holding audiences with courtiers, issuing orders dispatching troops on expeditions, and holding festival celebrations. The hall is the tallest and most magnificent hall in the Forbidden City.

The Hall, which sits on an 8.13 m tall three-tiered white marble terrace, is 11 bays wide (60.01 m) and five bays deep (33.33 m). The structure, which is 37.44 m in height and has a platform area covering 2,377 $m^2$, has a hipped roof with double eaves and yellow glazed tiles. The bracket sets under the upper eaves are projected four tiers and those under the lower eaves, three tiers. They are arranged in the highest rank. The interior of the hall includes 72 Phoebe nanmu columns. The gold lacquered throne with carved dragons in the centre of the hall symbolizes the absolute power of the emperor. The throne is surrounded by six gold lacquered columns with carved dragons on the shafts and is backed by a grand gold lacquered screen with seven linked panels representing supremacy and nobility.

1. Inscribed board of the Hall of Supreme Harmony
2. Main ridge finial with dragon pattern
3. Small mythological figure ornaments
4. Decorative coloured paintings
5. Sloping ridge beast ornaments
6. Bracket sets
7. Column
8. Platform

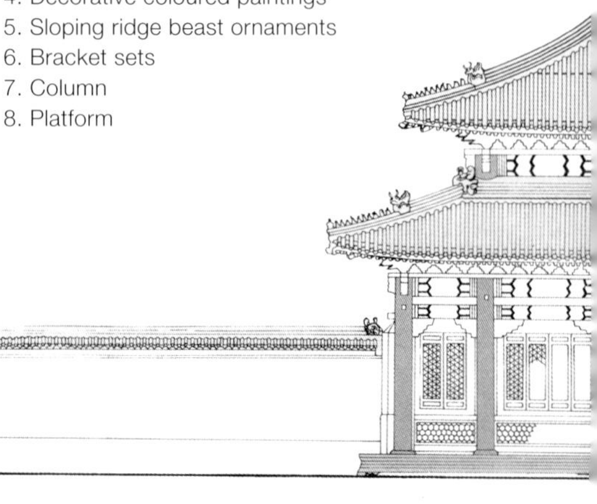

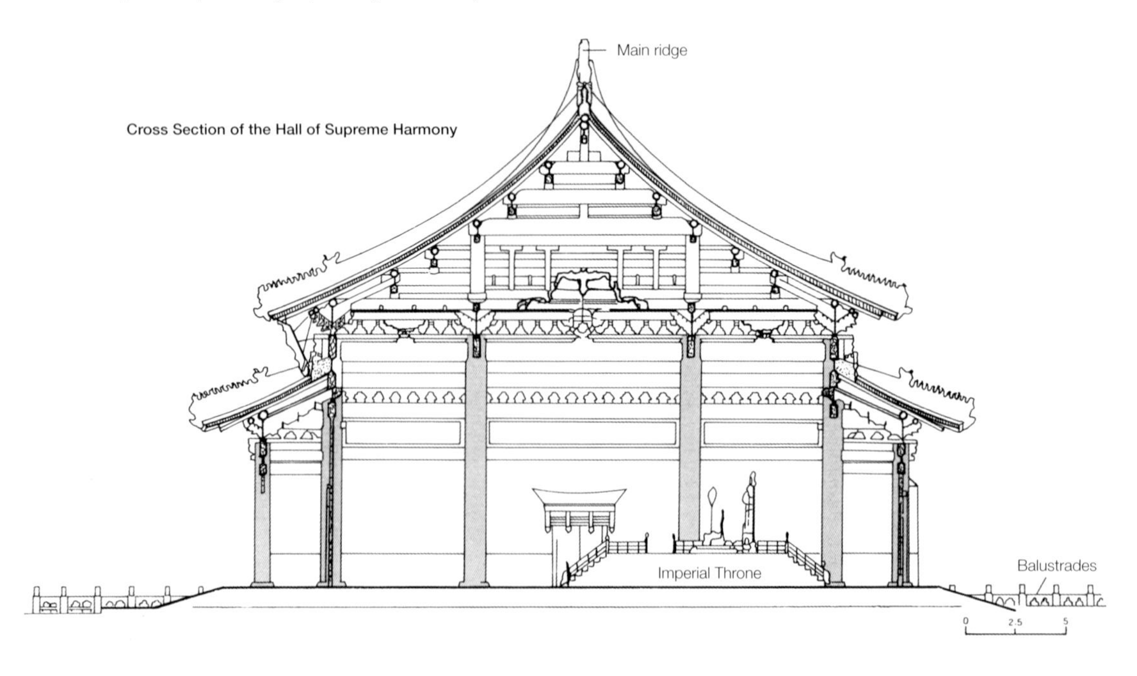

Cross Section of the Hall of Supreme Harmony

Section of the Hall of Supreme Harmony

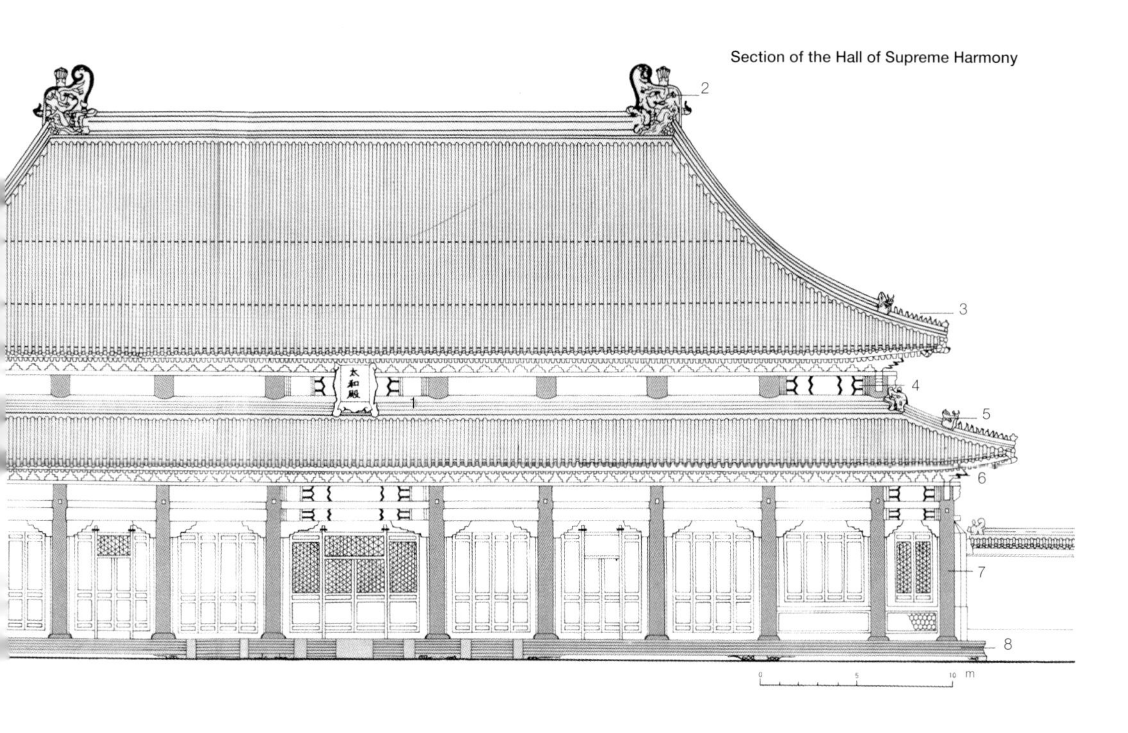


Plan of the Hall of supreme Harmony

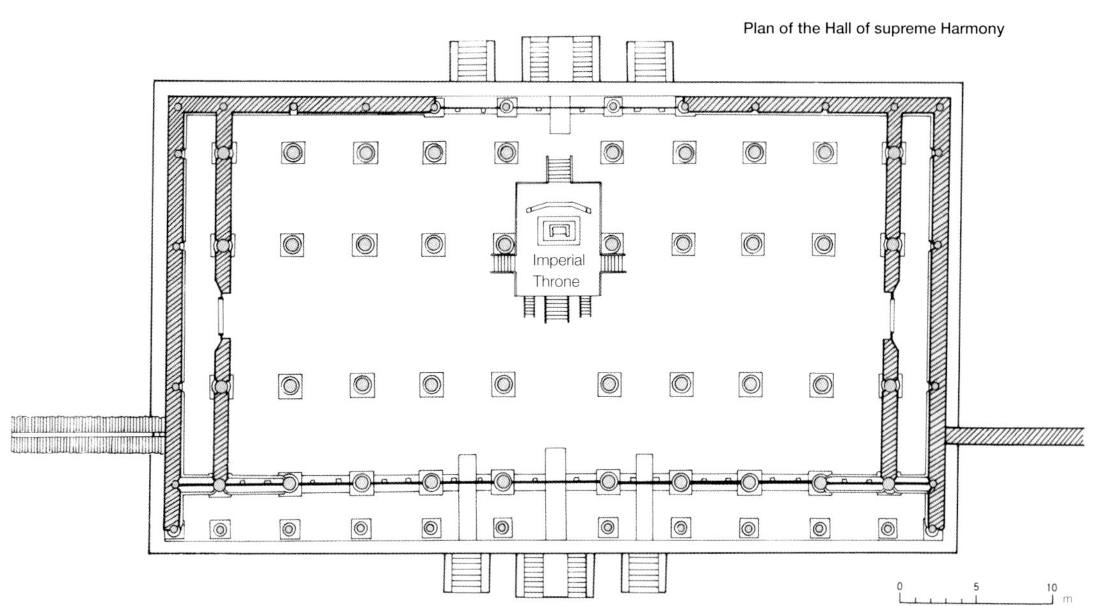

## Southwestern View of the Hall of Supreme Harmony

The Hall of Supreme Harmony is not only the largest hall in the Forbidden City, but also the largest extant wood structure in China. The hall was built in 1420, or the 18th year in the Yongle reign of Ming Emperor Chengzu. The structure was repeatedly destroyed by fire in intervening years and was rebuilt during the 34th year of the Kangxi reign of Qing Emperor Shizu. The ornate Hall of Supreme Harmony sits on a three-tiered marble terrace rising eight m in height. A Jialiang (a bronze standard grain measure housed in a pavilion-like stone stand) and a stone sundial on the terrace symbolize the balance of power under heaven. The expansive courtyard and three-tiered terrace stress the supreme position of the hall, and implies the total supremacy of the emperor.

## Bronze Tortoise Fronting the Hall of Supreme Harmony

The Hall of Supreme Harmony sits on a three-tiered terrace filled with objects. The objects include a Jialiang (a standard grain measure housed in a stone stand) and a sundial which represent the balance of power under heaven, as well as a cast bronze tortoise and crane which are not only renown for their decorative and aesthetic value, but also imply the emperor's wish for longevity. A lid in the back of the hollow body and holes in the mouth of the tortoise served a special ceremonial purpose. Rosin, agalloch eaglewood and pine boughs stuffed into the body of the bronze tortoise and crane were burned during grand ceremonies held in the Hall of Supreme Harmony. Smoke wafting from the mouths of the objects filled the air with a delicate fragrance, and not only added a surreal touch to the atmosphere, but also accentuated the solemnity of the occasion.

## Dehorned Dragon Gargoyles on the Three-tiered Terrace of the Hall of Supreme Harmony

The three great halls in the outer court—Hall of Supreme Harmony, Hall of Complete Harmony and Hall of Preserving Harmony—are a sight to behold. The structures stand one behind the other on an H-shaped terrace composed of three stacked Sumeru tiers rising 8.13 m in height. Each pedestal is bordered by marble balustrades with 1,458 upright marble posts in between, with globular caps bearing carved cloud-and-dragon tracery symbolizing the Son of Heaven. Chi in Chinese is represented by a dehorned dragon-like beast which was believed to protect life and property from fire. Hence, gargoyles in the shape of dehorned dragon heads are found underneath the marble posts on every tier of the terrace. Runoff diverted through the gargoyles on rainy days made it appear as if a thousand dragons were venting their fury.

**Golden-Dragon Hexi Decorative Paintings on Beams, Lintels and Bracket Sets** / left

Gilded dragons and other decorative patterns found in the Hall of Supreme Harmony belong to the hexi style, the highest grade decorative painting characterized by the general use of gold and likenesses of dragons symbolizing imperial power. The bracket sets under the lower eaves of the hall have three projecting tiers-single tier of qiao and double tiers of ang, one tier less than those under the upper eaves. The interior parts of bracket sets extend upward to the principal purlins, as were the vogue during the Qing Dynasty. Golden patterns of dragons covering all exposed wood members in the Hall of Supreme Harmony transform the hall into a veritable world of dragons.

**Caisson in the Hall of Supreme Harmony** / right

The caisson in the Hall of Supreme Harmony is supported by four gilded columns decorated with dragon patterns. The square lower section of the caisson serves as a base around which bracket sets are laid on the four sides to carry the load from above. The intermediate section is an octagonal drum surrounded by a series of triangles and rhomboids formed by cross beams and decorated with dragon-and-phoenix patterns. The round caisson upper section is encircled by tiny bracket sets to which bear the weight of the round cover plate, or mirror. A coiled dragon holding a "holy pearl" in its teeth is etched into the centre of the mirror. The stateliness and luxuriousness of the gilded caisson is enhanced by a green and blue coffered ceiling.

**Interior of the Hall of Supreme Harmony** / opposite page

Six round columns, all covered with gold lacquer and decorated with powder-dribbled and gold-leafing serpentine dragons, form a patronizing array around the throne in the Hall of Supreme Harmony. The throne, which is also finished with gold lacquer and sits atop a seven step staircase, is the heaviest, largest, most elaborately carved and most elegantly ornamented throne in the Forbidden City. Three dragon sculptures form the back of the throne. A Sumeru dais abutting a seven-paneled screen replaces legs beneath the throne. The throne is surrounded by elephants bearing Heavenly vases to symbolize peace under heaven; a unicorn to symbolize the virtue of the monarch and the support he commanded from a host of talented people; celestial cranes and incense burners signifying longevity.

## Decorative Gable of the Hall of Preserving Harmony / left

Qing Dynasty emperors used the Hall of Preserving Harmony to fete members of the imperial family and husbands of princesses during their weddings. Imperial exams had been held in the hall since the years under the reign of Emperor Qianlong. The hall, which is slightly below the Hall of Supreme Harmony in terms of architectural grade, has a double-eaved gable-and-hipped roof. The gables on important buildings in the Forbidden City were painstakingly decorated to indicate their imperial status. Gables on the roof of the Hall of Preserving Harmony are decorated with golden coin-and-ribbon patterns against a vermilion background. The combination of patterns on gables intertwined with hexi decorative paintings under the eaves shines resplendently in the sunshine and is indeed a unique ornamental feature of imperial buildings.

## A Corner of Eaves in the Palace of Heavenly Purity / right

The Palace of Heavenly Purity, a major building in the Inner Court, served as the imperial living quarters and is therefore embellished with higher grade ornamentation. The fact that structure features the same double-eaved hipped roof as the Hall of Supreme Harmony indicates its eminent position amongst halls and palaces in the Inner Court. Hexi paintings on the underside of eaves represent the highest grade of colour decoration. Central parts, or fang xin, of tie-beams joining peripteral columns to interior columns in the eave gallery depict dragons in running or sitting postures. The gallery's coffered ceiling is also emblazoned with patterns of sitting dragons. The decorative paintings with dragon patterns are repeated with powder-dribbling and gold-leafing to glamorize the entire exterior of the hall. The graphic and graceful dragons appear ready to soar into the blue sky at any moment.

## Hall of Complete Harmony, Hall of Preserving Harmony and Balustrades on the Three-tiered Terrace / next page

The three great halls were constructed slightly different from each other to comply with the hierarchical system of imperial architecture, with the Hall of Supreme Harmony being the primary structure in the Forbidden City. The Hall of Complete Harmony, a temporary rest stop for the emperor, is a five-bay-square structure surrounded by an arcade and topped by a single-eaved pyramidal roof. The Hall of Preserving Harmony, which ranks just below the Supreme Harmony in terms of architectural grade, features a double-eaved gable-and-hipped roof and nine bay facade. The three halls, laid out on the central axis, form the centrepiece of the Forbidden City.

## The Hall of Union

Although similar is design to the Hall of Complete Harmony, the Hall of Union is smaller and does not have a surrounding gallery. The hall, which is laid out on a square platform, is three bays wide and has a pyramidal roof, each sloping ridge of which is ornamented with seven statuettes of beasts. The wives of high officials and imperial concubines visited the hall to pay tribute to the empress. The gates and windows of the hall, built during the Jiajing reign of the Ming Dynasty, are embellished with dragon and phoenix patterns in a variety of colours. The unique decorative style of the Hall of Union purportedly reveals the hall's unique position in the Forbidden City.

## Timber-framed Construction of The Hall of Supreme Harmony

Ancient Chinese buildings feature numerous complicated external forms, while internal structures are simply combinations of structural members such as columns, beams, lintels, web plates, purlins, bracket sets, rafters, roof sheathings, etc. Different combinations of structural members form various types of wood structures such as hipped roofs, gable-and-hipped roofs and pyramidal roof structures.

The Hall of Supreme Harmony, the highest in rank and system of existing ancient Chinese wood structures, has the most expansive floor area with a width of eleven bays and a depth of five bays. The structure is topped with a double-eaved hipped roof. There are six rows of columns with 12 columns each. The 72 columns are arranged in a neat and simplified grid. The brilliant and imposing beams and bracket sets are painted with imperial hexi decorative patterns on blue-green bases and with the golden colour as the main tone. The structural system of the Hall is clear and precise. All simplified structural members are linked by a simple and stable tenon-and-mortise system.

1. Peristyle column
2. Peripteral column under upper eaves
3. Hypostyle column
4. Upper lintel
5. Lower lintel
6. Web plate between lintels
7. Tie-beam under peach-point beam
8. Peach-point beam
9. Plate carrying bracket sets
10. Lintel under upper eaves
11. Lintel carrying lower-eave rafters
12. Running-horse panel
13. Eaves purlin
14. Purlin under projecting eaves
15. Seven-purlin beam
16. Tie-beam under the main beam
17. Five-purlin beam
18. Three-purlin beam
19. Short post
20. Double-panel beam
21. Single-panel beam

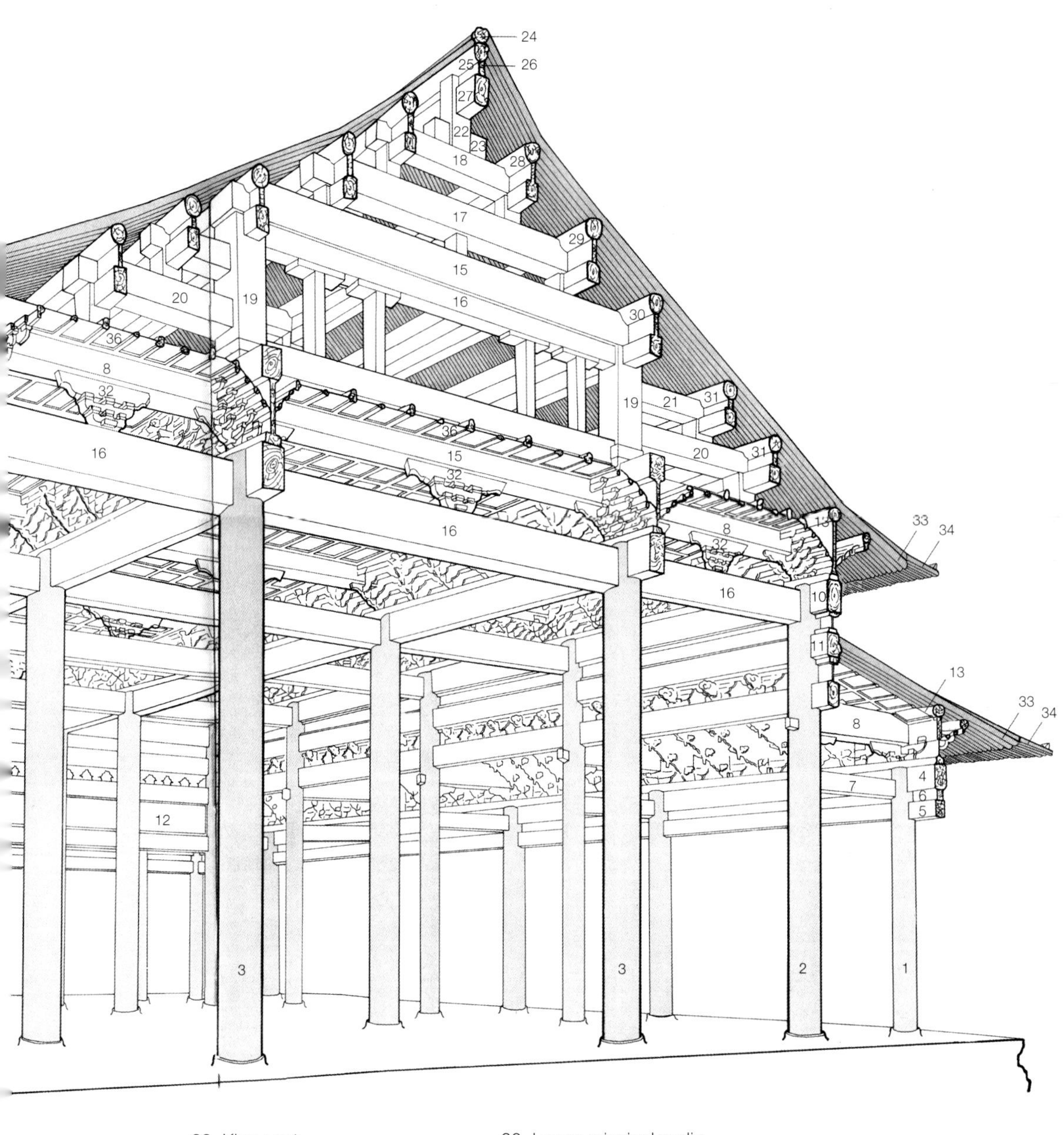


22. King post
23. King-post-fixing piece
24. Ridge supporter
25. Ridge purlin
26. Web-plate to ridge purlin
27. Ridge tie-beam
28. Upper principal purlin
29. Intermediate principal purlin
30. Lower principal purlin
31. Principal purlin
32. Intervallic bracket set
33. Eaves rafter
34. Flying rafter
35. Bracket set with end stretched beneath principal purlin
36. Coffered ceiling

## Bridal Chamber in the Palace of Earthly Tranquility

The Palace of Earthly Tranquility, located in the third row of halls in the inner court, served as the sleeping quarters for the empress. The palace features a double-eaved hipped roof similar to that of the Palace of Heavenly Purity, with one noticeable difference being that each sloping roof ridge has only seven animal statuettes. Walls in the eastern chamber of the palace, which served as the bridal chamber on the emperor's wedding day, are painted with red lacquer, and lanterns inscribed with Chinese character meaning "double happiness" hang from the ceiling and above the red-laquered door. Two wood screen walls, one standing along the path leading from the inner gate of the Palace of Earthly Tranquility to the eastern chamber and another in the hallway on the eastern side of the chamber itself, bear the same Chinese characters.

## Interior of the Hall of Union

The Hall of Union, situated between the Palace of Heavenly Purity and the Palace of Earthly Tranquility, provided the empress with a venue for receiving tribute on festive occasions. Qing Dynasty law dictated that the empress was in charge of internal affairs. Despite that fact, however, internal affairs were actually handled by the Board of Domestic Affairs. For example, the empress had no control over 25 imperial seals of power housed in the Hall of Union following the death of Emperor Qianlong. A grandfather clock stands in the western section of the hall and Chinese clepsydrae, timepieces from ancient China, are found in the eastern section. (Photo by Hu Chui)

## The Palace of Heavenly Purity

The Hall of Heavenly Purity, which housed the primary sleeping chambers of Ming emperors, was constructed in the 18th year in the Yongle reign of the Ming Dynasty and was repeatedly refurbished in ensuing years. The extant hall was rebuilt during the Jiajing reign of the Ming Dynasty. Qing emperors used the palace for various purposes, including sleeping chambers, reading room and forum for issuing instructions on memorials submitted to the throne. Emperor Yongzheng moved his sleeping chambers to the Hall of Mental Cultivation, with emperors thereafter using the Palace of Heavenly Purity as a site for receiving envoys from foreign countries. The hall, which is nine bays wide and has a double-eaved hipped roof, sits on a single tier stone terrace. A corridor linked to the Gate of Heavenly Purity eliminated the need for a stairway at the entrance of the hall. The Hall of Heavenly Purity is quite different from the solemn Hall of Supreme Harmony in that it evokes congeniality appropriate to the inner court of the imperial family's residential quarters.

## Throne in the Palace of Heavenly Purity / next page

The hall served roughly the same purpose as halls in the outer court dictated the installation of a throne similar to those found in the Hall of Supreme Harmony and Hall of Preserving Harmony. A three step wooden staircase leads to the throne which is backed by an ornate five-paneled screen. Incense burners, tripods and bronze cranes sit on either side of the throne, and both it and the screen are decorated with gilded dragon patterns. A horizontal board hanging above the throne bears a four Chinese character inscription reading "Justice and Uprightness". A box hidden behind the board held the name of the successor to the throne. (Photo by Hu Chui)

弘敷五典無輕民事惟難
惟精惟一

正大光明
表正萬邦慎厥身脩思永
克寬克仁皇建其有極

## The Pavilion of Ten Thousand Springs

The Pavilion of One Thousand Autumns and the Pavilion of Ten Thousand Springs, which are similar in design and arrangement and comply with the architectural style of the Imperial Garden, sit symmetrically on either side of the Hall of Imperial Peace. Both pavilions were built in 1536, or the 15th year in the Jiajing reign of the Ming Dynasty. Porticos protruding from four sides of each pavilion transform the otherwise square plan into a cross. The structures have double-eaved roofs, with lower eaves forming a square and upper eaves a conical top to embody the ancient theory that heaven is round and the earth square. Although similar, the two pavilions differ slightly in terms of decorative detail. Nonetheless, both were constructed in strict accordance with the standards of imperial architecture. The monotony of yellow glazed-tile roofs, the quintessential of Chinese style imperial architecture, is remedied by the lively shapes of the plans and roofs.

## Pavilion of Imperial Prospect Atop the Hill of Piled Excellence

opposite page

The Imperial Garden, located at the northern end of the central axis in the Forbidden City, afforded snug seclusion for the emperor and imperial concubines. The man-made Hill of Piled Excellence in the northeastern corner of the garden was built during the Wanli reign of the Ming Dynasty. Well-designed caves are strategically located along the slopes of the tall and elegant hill. A pathway on the eastern slope leads to the top of the hill, and a flight of stone steps threads its way through the series of caves to the Pavilion of Imperial Prospect on the summit. The Pavilion of Imperial Prospect, a small square structure with a four-cornered pyramidal roof, provides a breathtaking panoramic view of the array of yellow glazed-tile roofs in the Forbidden City and the western hills looming on the horizon.

## A Caisson in the Pavilion of Auspicious Clarity

The Pavilion of Auspicious Clarity, situated in the northwestern corner of the Imperial Garden, was built in 1583, or the 11th year of the Wanli reign of the Ming Dynasty. The ceiling is decorated with dragon patterns and is supported by a centre caisson. The square lower section is ringed by an octagonal ring of brackets. and the upper circular section is decorated with wood carvings of serpentine dragons. The circular caisson is also ornamented with a pair of gold-lacquered wood dragons frolicking with a pearl. Caissons commonly found in pavilions and halls throughout the Forbidden City are most often ornamented with gilded dragon and phoenix patterns. The Pavilion of Auspicious Clarity is unique in that its gilded caisson supports the blue and green ceiling.

## Gate of Mental Cultivation / opposite upper

The palace complexes in the Forbidden City are separated by high walls and linked by a series of gates. Most portals in important courtyards and various halls and palaces in the Inner Court are topped by glazed-tile roofs. Portals, which are built of bricks and covered with glazed tiles, feature brackets, beams, rafter ends and purlins under the eaves in imitation wood members decorated in xuanzi style. Structures of this type are more sturdy than wooden structures and are more colourful and lively than masonry. The four corners and centre of the wall on either side of portals are ornamented with glazed tiles arranged in decorative patterns. Gates of portals are fashioned from solid wood imbedded with 81 knobs. The centre and four corners of a glazed-tile screen wall erected by either side of the Portal and slightly lower than it, is also ornamented with glazed tiles and stands on a Sumeru base.

## Portico of the Hall of Mental Cultivation / opposite lower

The Hall of Mental Cultivation was initially constructed during the Ming Dynasty and was rebuilt during the Yongzheng reign of the Qing Dynasty. The hall served as the sleeping quarters for Emperor Shunzhi of the early Qing Dynasty. The hall was also used as a venue for handling state affairs and receiving officials and as a result acquired a status similar to that of the Palace of Heavenly Purity. The H-shaped Hall of Mental Cultivation includes a front hall where the emperor handled government affairs, with a short corridor to the north leading to the rear hall which the emperor used as a rest area. The front hall, which has nine-bay-wide facade, measures 36 m in width and 5 m in depth. A portico is found between the front central bay and the western sub-central bay. The rear hall covers nine bays and is topped by a gabled roof with round ridges. The photo offers a glimpse of the Hall of Mental Cultivation.

養心門
请勿攀登
跨越栏杆
请勿攀登
跨越栏杆

## The Room of Three Rarities

The Room of Three Rarities, a tiny partitioned room providing access to the western chamber of the Hall of Mental Cultivation was originally known as the Room of Warmth in the Hall of Mental Cultivation. The present name was derived from the fact that it housed the "three rarities"—three famous calligraphic copybooks collected by the emperor during the Qianlong reign of the Qing Dynasty. The works include Wang Xizhi's A Sunny Day After a Snowstorm (Kuaixue Shiqing Tie); Wang Xianzhi's Mid-Autumn; and Wang Xun's Copybook Dedicated to Boyuan. Emperor Qianlong, however, interpreted the term "three rarities" to mean rare talent, rare sage and rare Heaven. Horizontal boards and a scroll inscribed with the text of the essay "Notes on the Room of Three Rarities" in Emperor Qianlong's own handwriting hang on the walls in the Room of Three Rarities.

## The Pavilion of the Rain of Flowers / opposite page

The Pavilion of the Rain of Flowers, built during the reign of Qing Emperor Qianlong, is a three-storied structure with portals on each side of the ground floor. The columns on the ground floor feature knobs carved with the faces of animals, while columns on the second and third floors feature bud-shaped capitals inscribed with gilded dragons. The roof, which is covered with gilded-bronze cylindrical and plain tiles, has four ridges ornamented with a gilded bronze dragon and is capped by a cupola in the shape of a pagoda. The pavilion is well-known for its enamel mandala which enshrines a statue of tantric Buddhism. The mandala, built during the 20th year of the reign of Emperor Qianlong, stands on a round white marble pedestal and is covered by a hardword case in the design of a pavilion with a double-eaved pyramidal roof. The elegant mandala, built of metal-inlaid enamel, is highly representative of superb craftsmanship.

華滋堂

倚蹕九重臺香莚萬
壽杯依旬初降雨三
月旱聞雷露結朝隮
密葉含宿雨開幸承
天澤豫湯使日光催
同雲接野烟飛雪舞
長天拂蘚添梅色潤
樓助粉妍光含班氏
扇韵入楚王經六出
迎仙藻千箱答瑞年
唐臣李嶠喜雨喜雪
律詩
臣潘祖蔭敬書

亭亭如意

## Rear Bedroom Chamber in the Hall of Mental Cultivation / preceding page

Two small curtained doors in the wall behind the throne in the Hall of Mental Cultivation open to a short corridor linking the front and rear halls and lead to the emperor's bedroom. The middle three rooms in a row of five bedrooms in the Hall of Mental Cultivation are interlinked. The central room is furnished with a bed and chairs for the emperor's personal use. The room to the east features a throne and benches made of red sandalwood, while the room to the west is furnished with a red sandalwood cabinet carved with cloud and dragon patterns and a kang where the emperor could sit and relax, as well as antiques, calligraphic scrolls, paintings and other rare treasures. The bedrooms on the eastern and western ends of the row are each furnished with a kang, or "dragon's bed". Partition doors and furniture in the two rooms are made of expensive hardwood. The short corridor links the bedrooms directly to the front hall. (Photo by Hu Chui)

## Interior of the Hall of Manifest Origin

The Hall of Manifest Origin, one of the West Six Palaces, is located south of the Palace of Eternal Spring and north of the Hall of Supremacy. The hall was built on the site of the Gate of Eternal Spring which stood during the Jiaqing reign of Qing Emperor Renzong. A three-bay-wide portal on the north side of the hall served as a stage which was the venue for nine days of theatrical performances in celebration of Empress Dowager Cixi's 50th birthday. The interior of the Hall of Manifest Origin is ornamented with a suspended screen sided by balustrades and a central opening, as well as an overhanging frame with two partition doors on either side. Glass lanterns in a double-square design hang from the ceiling. The hall's collection of antiques includes a pair of jade carvings known for their smooth and glossy appearance, several traditional Chinese calligraphic and painted scrolls, and two tiny screens inscribed with landscape paintings. (Photo by Hu Chui)

## The Palace of Eternal Spring

The Palace of Eternal Spring, one of the West Six Palaces, was initially built during the Yongle reign of the Ming Dynasty and was rebuilt in 1683, or the 22nd year of the reign of Qing Emperor Kangxi. The palace served as the residence of High Consort Hu of Ming Emperor Xuande, High Consort Li of Ming Emperor Tianqi and Empress Xiaoxian, the wife of Emperor Qianlong of the Qing Dynasty. The Gate of Eternal Spring in front of the palace was demolished in the 15th year in the Jiaqing reign of the Qing Dynasty to make room for the Hall of Manifest Origin, a five-bay-wide structure. The rear portal features a three-bay-wide round-ridged roof which was used as a tiny stage. Empress Dowager Cixi had lived in this palace for a period of time after Emperor Tongzhi ascended to the throne in the late Qing Dynasty. Emperor Guangxu and Puyi also lived in the palace.

## The Hall of Imperial Supremacy

The Hall of Imperial Supremacy, the front hall of the Palace of Tranquil Longevity architectural complex, like the Palace of Tranquil Longevity, was the residence of Emperor Qianlong after he had abdicated the throne as the incumbent emperor's father. Similar to the Palace of Heavenly Purity and the Palace of Earthly Tranquility in architectural design, the nine-bay hall sits on a stone terrace skirted with marble balustrades, and is linked to the Gate of Tranquil Longevity by a six-metre-wide stone elevated way, 1.6 m in height. The hall, which features a hipped roof, is rated slightly below the Hall of Supreme Harmony in architectural grade. However, its interior and exterior fittings are roughly ornamented with the same patterns of gilded dragons and hexi paintings. The decorated corbels projecting from columns to support lintels are carved with gold-lacquered dragons with heads protruding from the surface, a design common to structures built during the reign of Emperor Qianlong.

## Stone Screen Fronting the Palace of Great Benevolence

The Palace of Great Benevolence, one of the East Six Palaces which sits south of the Palace of Inheriting Heaven, was named as the Palace of Everlasting Peace when completed during the Yongle reign of the Ming Dynasty. The present name was adopted during the 14th year of the Jiajing reign of the Ming Dynasty. The palace, rebuilt during the Shunzhi reign of the Qing Dynasty, is laid out in the fashion of two adjoined courtyards with a hall in front and a palace in the rear. Just as the East and West Six Palaces, a screen wall is found at the entrance to the Palace of Great Benevolence. Chinese architecture often featured a screen wall erected at the entrance of a building to shield the interior from public view. The screen wall also serves to add variety and depth to the space. Most screen walls in the East and West Six Palaces are wooden structures. However, the screen wall in the Hall of Great Benevolence is an exception.

## The Gate of Imperial Supremacy

The Gate of Imperial Supremacy, built in 1688, or the 27th year of the Kangxi reign of the Qing Dynasty, serves as the entrance to the palace complex which consists of the Palace of Tranquil Longevity and the Hall of Imperial Supremacy. The height of the wall makes the Gate unique from other courtyard gates in the Forbidden City. As a rule, the awnings are ornamented with protruding glazed-tile eaves, and brackets and horizontal beams and rafters below the eaves are covered with glazed tiles covered with xuanzi patterns and arranged in the fashion of a mosaic. The entire structure, which sits on a stone Sumeru base, is ornamented with felicity. A glazed-tile screen wall imbedded with the likenesses of nine glazed dragons stands opposite to the entrance hall. This nine-dragon screen wall in the Forbidden City is the namesake of its counterpart in Beihai Park.

## Narrow Lane Leading to the Palace of Tranquil Longevity

Walls separate the host of building complexes in the Forbidden City, including the three great halls in the outer court, the palaces in the Inner Court, the East and West Six Palaces, and the complex of the Palace of Tranquil Longevity. For example, the Western lane separates the Inner Court from the Palace of Gathering Excellence, the Hall of Manifest Harmony and the Palace of Emperor's Assistance. In terms of the West Six Palaces, the Second Western Lane separates the Palace of Gathering Excellence, the Hall of Manifest Harmony, the Palace of Emperor's Assistance and the Palace of Eternal Longevity from the Palace of Complete Happiness, the Palace of Eternal Spring and the Hall of Manifest Origin. The photo captures a glimpse of a narrow lane west of the Palace of Tranquil Longevity.

## The Palace of Tranquil Longevity

The Palace of Tranquil Longevity is patterned after the Palace of Earthly Tranquility, but is rated at a lower architectural grade. Both palaces are duplicates of the Palace of Purity and Tranquility in the Qing Palace of the Prosperous Capital (the Imperial Palace in Shenyang). The Palace of Tranquil Longevity is topped by a single-eaved gable-and-hipped roof, with frontal eaves supported by square columns ornamented with dragon-and-phoenix hexi decorative paintings. Decorative perforate boards and queti (carved corbels supporting lintel ends) are graced with gold-lacquered dragon patterns. The palace's interior decor is in the same fashion as the Palace of Earthly Tranquility.

## Tiny Theatrical Stage in the Study of Peaceful Old Age

As its name suggests, the Forbidden City was heavily guarded from the outside world, and even the most favored ladies in the imperial court were prohibited from leaving its confines without permission. Therefore, theatrical stages were built in a number of palaces behind the walls to entertain the emperors, empresses and a large retinue of concubines. The stage in the Study of Peaceful Old Age is a wooden structure in the shape of a tiny pavilion with bamboo fences erected on the western side. The stage's overhead canopy is painted with the likeness of a violet trellis. The landscape painting on the western wall behind the stage portrays lotus flowers in a pond, and the northern wall is covered with a painting of pavilions and chambers. The decorations combine to form the backdrop for the stage and serve to enliven the atmosphere. A two-floor pavilion sits opposite the stage, and thrones for the emperor are found on both floors. (Photo by Hu Chui)

## Cup-floating Stream in the Pavilion of the Ceremony of Purification

The Pavilion of the Ceremony of Purification situated in the western section of the front courtyard of the Garden of the Palace of Tranquil Longevity. Ancient scholars gathered on the banks of the stream on the first si day (si is the sixth of the twelve Earthly Branches for designating days) of the third lunar month (the date was changed to the third of the third lunar month after the Wei Dynasty), and a cup placed on the stream was allowed to float downstream. The cup eventually came to rest and the man in front of whom it stopped was asked to drink the wine in the cup and improvise a poem. Hence the name, Cup-Floating Stream. Water was drawn from a well at the Gate of Spreading Happiness into a giant vat and was diverted through a channel and flowed down rockery into the Cup-Floating Stream in the pavilion. It was drained from the stream through a channel at the foot of a rockery to the north of the pavilion into the imperial drainage ditch. (Photo by Hu Chui)

## Panoramic View of the East Five Lodges

The East Five Lodges, also known as the East Five Heavenly Lodges, are located north of the East Six Palaces. Each lodge consists of three main halls and four ancillary halls arranged in a quadrangle which contains three courtyards. In ancient time, the lodges occupied by the children and grandchildren of the royal family and eunuchs responsible for their wellbeing. As a child, Qing Emperor Jiaqing and his attendants lived in Lodges Number One and Two. Somewhat later, when the imperial sons and grandsons were moved to the Three Southern Lodges, the East Five Lodges were converted into offices used by eunuchs to handle management affairs, warehouses for crowns, robes, belts, shoes, ornaments, mosquito nets used by the emperor, antiques and utensils, and studios for hired painters. The East Five Lodges, which are separated from the Imperial Garden by a wall, sit symmetrically with the West Five Lodges across from the complex of West Six Palaces. (Photo by Hu Chui)

## Pavilion of Pleasant Sounds / opposite page

The large number of festivals necessitated the construction of a host of stages and the employment of professional troupes. The largest stage in the Forbidden City is found in the Pavilion of Pleasant Sounds east of the Hall of Spiritual Cultivation. The three-floor stage, which was named for the Stage of Longevity, Stage of Good Fortune, and Stage of Happiness, are linked by a staircase, and each floor has its own entrances and exits. The stage on the first floor is the largest, and the third floor stage the smallest. Each stage has a layer of eaves with a round-ridged gable-and-hipped roof covered with yellow-glazed tiles on the top. This structure differs from its counterparts in the Forbidden City in that its peripteral columns are painted green. A horizontal board, painted black and inscribed with golden characters, hangs from frontal eaves on each stage.

### Interior of the Dome Behind the Hall of Bathing in Moral Integrity in the Hall of Military Eminence

A semi-circular dome and a four-square-metre floor paved with white glazed bricks sits behind the Hall of Bathing in Moral Integrity in the northwest corner of the Hall of Military Eminence. The walls are unusually thick to bear the weight of the domed roof, and the four corners of the walls feature a corbelled brick structure forming an enclosure which changes from an octagon into a cylinder. A hole 0.6 m in diameter on the centre of the dome provides ventilation and lighting. An arched passageway fashioned from white-glazed bricks to the south of the structure links it with the Hall of Bathing in Moral Integrity. A tiny round hole in the northern wall to provide access to hot-water supply equipment installed outside of the building. Water drainage holes are found in the floor.

### Pavilion of the Brookside in the Garden of the Palace of Compassion and Tranquility / opposite page

The Pavilion of the Brookside was built during the Ming Dynasty. The pavilion sits right to a bridge which spans an oblong pond. The pond, which is used to raise fish and grow lotus plants, extends to the eastern and western sides of the pavilion. Peonies and Chinese herbaceous peony plants are grown in two flower beds to the south and north of the pavilion which is tucked away in a cluster of pines, cypresses, Chinese catalpas, scholartrees, gingko trees and yulan magnolias. The doors and windows on four sides of the pavilion provide an excellent view of scenery in the garden. The sequestered peace and repose of the garden finds expression in an antithetical couplet by Emperor Qianlong,"During moments of leisure I can see cranes preening their feathers, and from time to time the tolling of bells can be heard from outside the yard."

## The Moat, City Wall and the Corner Watchtower

The wall surrounding the Forbidden City, 11.24 m in height, is built of bricks which were polished and air-dried to provide an appearance of smoothness and sturdiness. A 3,300 m long moat, which is 52 m wide and 6 m deep, runs along the foot of the wall. The moat, which is hemmed in between vertical stone banks topped with parapets, is paved with huge oblong stone slabs arranged in the fashion of a pipe to discourage people from crossing the moat during dry periods. Hence the name, Pipe River. The moat serves as the Forbidden City's first line of defence in a seemingly impregnable fortress which is also fortified with a high brick wall, towering gatetowers and the corner pavilions. The combination is the hallmark of the majestic, mystic and forbidden imperial palace.

## Corner Watchtower / opposite page

Watchtowers on each of the four corners of the wall are part of the defence works in the Forbidden City. Watchtowers, in the shape of a carpenter's square, have roofs with three layers of eaves. Eaves on the upper level are topped by a combination of a hipped quadruple roofs and gable-and-hipped roofs with gables on all four sides and upturned main ridges converging beneath gilded bulbous cupola. The lower eaves feature semi-pitched roof trusses. The watchtowers feature eight gable-and-hipped roofs with nine main ridges, with each watchtower boasting 72 ridges, 28 upturned corners, 10 richly ornamented gables, and 230 ridge ornaments in the shape of dragon heads. The watchtowers, which gleaming with captivating loveliness against the otherwise gloomy city wall and sparkling moat, evoke the essence of pavilions and chambers depicted in Song Dynasty paintings. Each watchtower is a masterpiece of ancient Chinese palatial architecture.

### Glazed-tile Ornaments on Gable Walls of the Chongzheng Hall

Though the main building on the central axis of the Imperial Palace in Shenyang, the Chongzheng Hall has a plain gabled roof instead of a more elaborate one, which shows that the more matured Han palatial style was yet to be adopted. Its importance is shown nevertheless by a number of glazed ceramics, like the roof covered with yellow glazed tiles and edged with green ones. The luxury and importance of an imperial building is also manifested by coloured glazed ridges, verge boards, and gable springers. It is quite different from the buildings in the Forbidden City, which are decorated with gold and coloured paintings.

## General Plan of the Imperial Palace in Shenyang

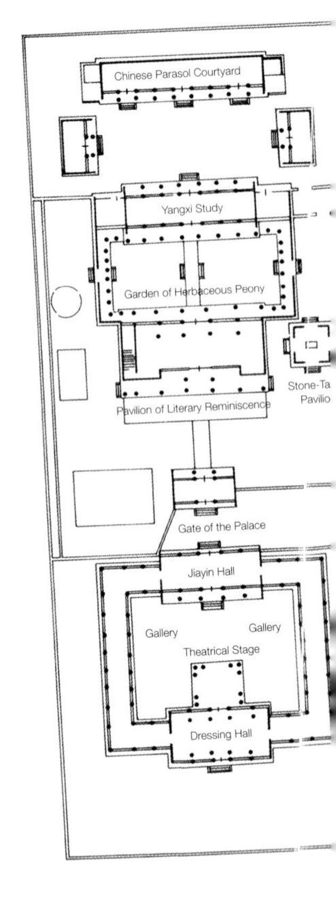


The Imperial Palace of Shenyang, located in the centre of the old city of Shenyang, Liaoning Province, was built by Nurhachi (Emperor Taizu) and Huangtaiji (Emperor Taizong) of the Qing Dynasty. Emperor Qianlong had it renovated many times. The palace we see today covers an area of 63,272.53 $m^2$ with a total floor space of 16,421.34 $m^2$, and has 96 buildings and 419 jian, or rooms.

The general layout of the Imperial Palace in Shenyang is divided into the East, Middle and West Sections. The architectural styles in the Middle and East Sections typify the style of palace architecture before the Manchus crossed the Great Wall and occupied Beijing. The Middle Section, which is the longest and widest among the three, has a road in front running from east to west with two memorial pailou (archways) called the Literary Virtue and the Military Merits. To the east of the Gate of Great Qing, the Imperial Ancestral Temple stands on a high terrace. On the axis starting from the Gate of Great Qing are the Chongzheng Hall, the Phoenix Tower, and the Palace of Purity and Tranquility.

The East Section is a long and narrow compound consisting of the Dazheng Hall and the Ten-Prince Pavilions. The Dazheng Hall stands on the north of the north-south axial line of the compound while the Ten-Prince Pavilions fan out in front. The two pavilions to the north are the Pavilions of the Left and Right Wing Princes; the other eight, arranged according to the order of the Eight Banners, are an expression of the Eight Banner system in palatial buildings. With the Dazheng Hall as the main building.

The Pavilion of Literary Reminiscence, the Jiayin Hall, and the Yangxi Study of the West Section were added during Qianlong's time. The Pavilion of Literary Reminiscence was an imperial library where *the Complete Collection in Four Treasures* (Si Ku Quan Shu) and *the Synthesis of Past and Present Books with Illustrations* (Gu Jin Tu Shu Ji Cheng) were housed. The Jiayin Hall and the Yangxi Study were where the emperors watched performances and studied.

## Section of the Chongzheng Hall

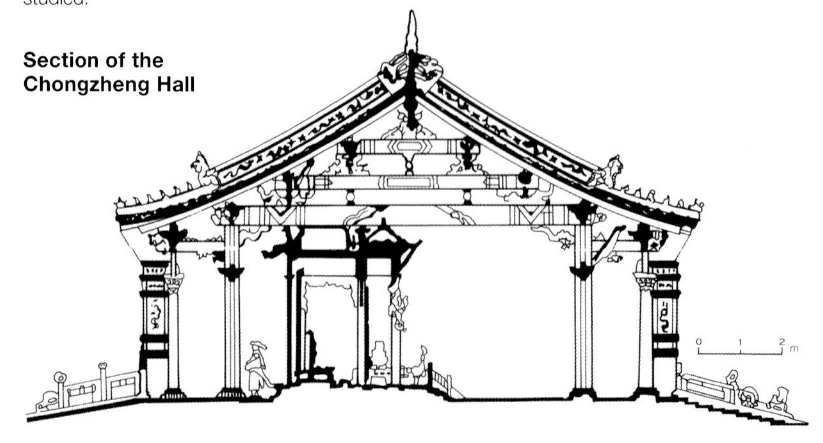

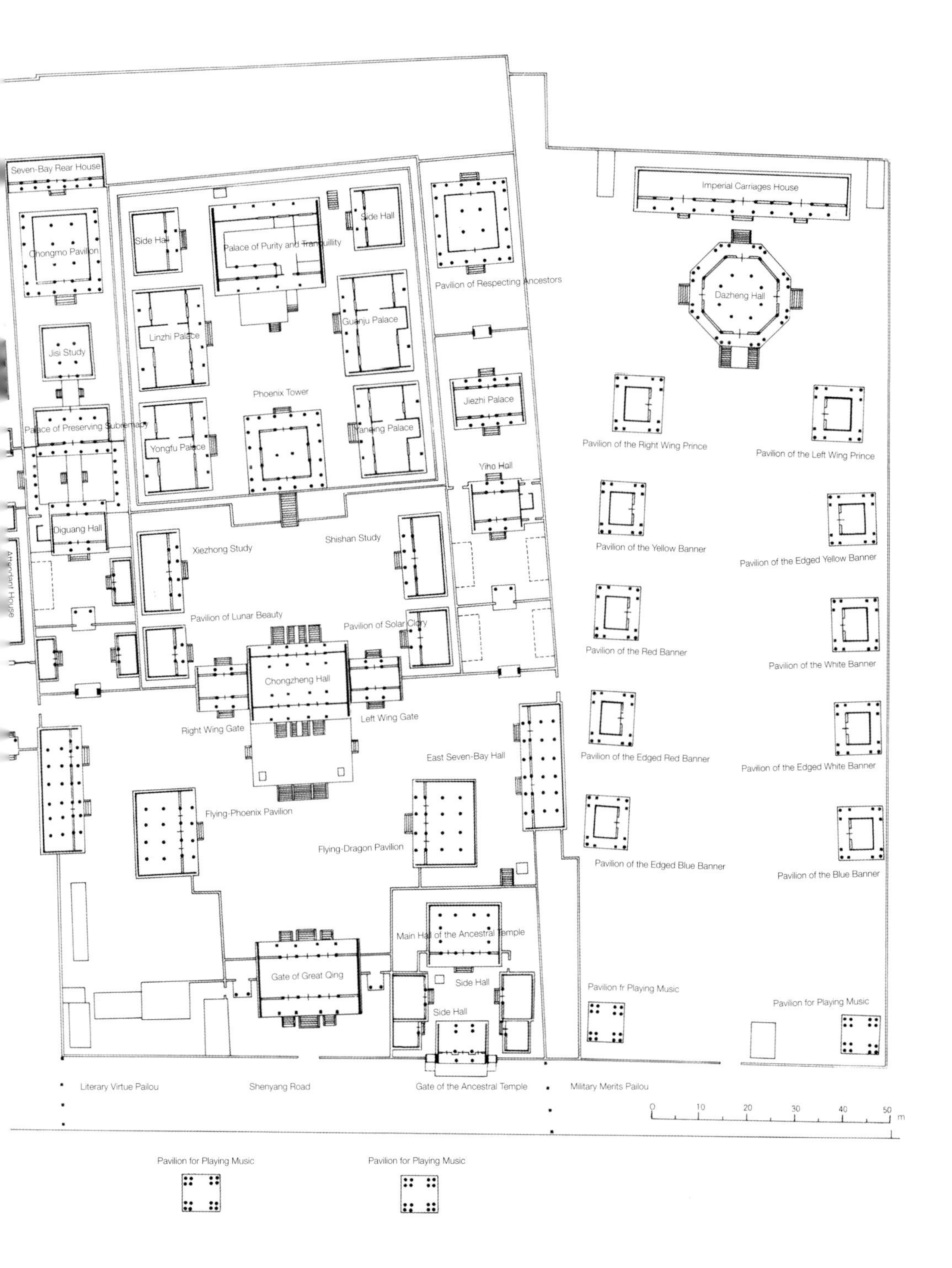
Seven-Bay Rear House
Imperial Carriages House
Side Hall
Side Hall
Palace of Purity and Tranquillity
Chongmo Pavilion
Pavilion of Respecting Ancestors
Dazheng Hall
Linzhi Palace
Guanju Palace
Jisi Study
Phoenix Tower
Jiezhi Palace
Palace of Preserving Supremacy
Yanqing Palace
Yongfu Palace
Pavilion of the Right Wing Prince
Pavilion of the Left Wing Prince
Yiho Hall
Diguang Hall
Xiezhong Study
Shishan Study
Pavilion of the Yellow Banner
Pavilion of the Edged Yellow Banner
Attendant House
Pavilion of Lunar Beauty
Pavilion of Solar Glory
Pavilion of the Red Banner
Pavilion of the White Banner
Chongzheng Hall
Right Wing Gate
Left Wing Gate
East Seven-Bay Hall
Pavilion of the Edged Red Banner
Pavilion of the Edged White Banner
Flying-Phoenix Pavilion
Flying-Dragon Pavilion
Pavilion of the Edged Blue Banner
Pavilion of the Blue Banner
Main Hall of the Ancestral Temple
Gate of Great Qing
Side Hall
Side Hall
Pavilion fr Playing Music
Pavilion for Playing Music
Literary Virtue Pailou
Shenyang Road
Gate of the Ancestral Temple
Military Merits Pailou
0
10
20
30
40
50
m
Pavilion for Playing Music
Pavilion for Playing Music

## Balustrades Fronting the Chongzheng Hall

Although the hall has a low-ranking gabled roof and is barely five bays wide, its importance is shown in its more elaborate decorations. Its partition doors with latticed sashes and skirt panels have high-ranking decorations and are painted vermilion, and the bronze fixtures are also decorated. The gable springers are faced with yellow and green glazed tiles. The terrace balustrades, including the posts, post heads, panels, and gargoyles all have dragon designs and patterns of plants. The picture shows the terrace balustrades, with their panels and post heads decorated with lively carvings of dragons. The panels are carved with running dragons and clouds, and the post heads are carved with whirling flowers and plants. They differ from the balustrades of marble in the Forbidden City in Beijing.

## Stone Carving Around the Flights of Steps Leading up to the Chongzheng Hall

Three flights of steps built of different kinds of stone in varied colours run up the Sumeru platform of the Chongzheng Hall at both the southern and the northern ends. In the centre is an imperial way with a bas-relief carving of two dragons frolicking with a pearl. Balustrades are erected at both sides of the flights and around the verandah of the hall. A striking combination of red, green, black, and white stones are used for the balustrades, posts, panels, and steps, as well as the drum-shaped stones at the lower end of the balustrades flanking the steps. The darkish-red steps of the two flights of steps at both sides seem to provide a red carpet. They enrich the colours as well as set off the imperial way in the centre. A stone animal sits in front of each of the drum-shaped stones—a rare combination in palatial buildings. The picture shows a drum-shaped stone and the animal of the flight of steps to the left.

## Sculptured Beam-ends on Peripteral Columns of the Chongzheng Hall

The decorations of wood-framed members of the verandahs in the front and back of the Chongzheng Hall differ from that of the Han style and show an influence of Tibetan architecture. The carved beam connecting the peripteral and the hypostyle columns is similar to that of the Gate of Great Qing: both are carved into dragons with their heads sticking out, their tails hidden in the hypostyle columns, their mouths open, and their claws reaching out. Their bodies, which are the beams themselves, are arched, and the dragons seem to be in the act of crawling out. This architectural style of the early Qing period combines art with the practical use of wooden members.

## Shrine Housing the Imperial Throne in the Chongzheng Hall / opposite page

The Chongzheng Hall was where Huangtaiji held audience with his ministers, and the shrine and throne are very elaborately decorated. The shrine, with a small protruding front, stands on a wooden dais. The shrine has everything that is needed for a wooden structure, including bracket sets, eaves, beams and columns, all covered with coloured paintings. A gilded descending dragon with its head raised coils around each of the two front columns where white and blue clouds float on a background of red. In the centre of the shrine is a throne and a fan-shaped screen decorated with a gilded dragon. In front of the throne are a desk, incense burners, and cranes, setting off the resplendent shrine and throne to the full.

念兹戎功用肇造我

## Wood Carving on Peripteral Column and Lintels of the Chongzheng Hall

The Imperial Palace in Shenyang is a complex built during the times of Nurhachi and Huangtaiji before the Manchus crossed the Great Wall. It is divided into the Middle, East and West Sections. The Chongzheng Hall is the main building of the Middle Section, with an obvious Tibetan architectural style. The picture shows a beam carved as a dragon crawling out from under the eaves, like the one in the Gate of Great Qing. Carvings with a regional flavor also decorate the column capital under the dragon's head.

## Wood Carving in Dragon Patterns under the Eaves of the Gate of Great Qing

opposite upper

The Gate of Great Qing is the main entrance to the Imperial Palace in Shenyang like the Meridian Gate of the Forbidden City in Beijing. It was where ministers waited for an audience with the emperor. The gate is five bays in width covered with a plain gabled roof. It has verandahs both in front and in the rear with square peripteral columns and round hypostyle columns. The beams connecting peripteral and hypostyle columns are carved into running dragons with their heads and front claws protruding beyond the peripteral columns and their tails inserted into the hypostyle columns. This kind of decoration differs from the Han style and has the flavor of Tibetan architecture. The peripteral columns are each capped with an animal-faced block surrounded by scroll designs, forming a common feature of Lamaist architecture.

## Beams and Columns of the Palace of Purity and Tranquility / opposite lower

The Han tradition of using a dragon to symbolize the emperor is widely used in palatial buildings. Inheriting this tradition, the Imperial Palace in Shenyang also has this symbolism carved on beams and columns. The exterior of the Palace of Purity and Tranquility is decorated with Shi-nian-yu (flaked-jade treatment) xuanzi paintings, the highest-rank xuanzi, second only to hexi paintings, with flower petals painted in blue and green alternatively in gradation. Although the palace was renovated many times, the demarcation lines on the beams still retain the style of early Qing. Unlike those in other halls in the Imperial Palace in Shenyang, the xuanzi paintings at the beam ends here are edged with strings of pearls or swastikas instead of designs with colour gradation, showing the prominence of the building.

## **Coffered Ceiling in the Phoenix Tower** / left

The Phoenix Tower is three stories high. The lower floor leads to the residential palaces. The intermediate and upper floors were where Huangtaiji feasted and rested. The tower also provides a good view of the surrounding scenery. It has no ceiling other than the inside of the roof with exposed rafters decorated with variations of lotus blossoms. The sheathing is painted with floating clouds and flowing waters. The purlins and beams are covered with a painting of precious pearls and passion flowers. The paintings on the beams still retain characteristics of the early Qing, not divided into sections of fang xin, zao tou and gu tou like those in the later Qing period. The phoenix patterns decorating the caisson in the upper story is enriched with auspicious clouds. As a whole, the decorative paintings in the Imperial Palace in Shenyang are more lively and varied than the more opulent ones in the Forbidden City in Beijing.

## **Interior Decorative Paintings on Beams and Other Members in the Chongzheng Hall** / right

The Chongzheng Hall has no ceiling other than the inside of the roof. The exposed beams of the roof are covered with hexi paintings. The fang xin, or the central part of the beam, is painted on a bas-relief carving of two dragons frolicking with a pearl. Floating clouds cover part of the dragons' bodies, and gilding is applied intermittently, in an economical way, as was the tradition of Yuan Dynasty paintings that the Qing had inherited. After two hundred years and several renovations the paintings still exhibit the style of the Qianlong period. But the paintings at zao tou, or the intervening parts, of the beams manifest the painting style of the early Qing period.

## The Phoenix Tower

Built when Huangtaiji expanded the Imperial Palace in Shenyang, this was the only new building that had bracket sets and three layers of eaves with a gable-and-hipped roof at the time. It is square in plan with three bays in width and depth surrounded by verandahs on its four sides. The roof is covered with yellow tiles and edged with green ones. The main ridge and the four sloping ridges atop the gablets are all decorated with running dragons, and both ends of the main ridge are decorated with dragon-shaped finials, holding the ridge ends in their mouths with their tails curled-up and with another blue-glazed descending dragons attached to. The sword handles on the backs of the dragon finials are shaped like flaming pearls. More lively and full of variety than the animal decorations on the ridges in the Forbidden City, they are another outstanding feature of the Imperial Palace in Shenyang. The tower was the highest building in the city of Shenyang in the beginning of the Qing Dynasty. From the top one can have a good view of the city.

## Interior of the Palace of Purity and Tranquility

The residential palace has high-ranking interior decorations on the beams and lintels. Two gilded dragons are painted on a red background decorated with floating clouds in a semi-circular section known as the baofu (wrapper). In the centre of the baofu is a flaming pearl. The square boards of the coffered ceiling are painted with circular dragon-phoenix patterns. The yellow joists with their meeting parts and the corners of the boards painted with blue and green patterns contrast sharply with the warm red. Although the paintings are not as splendid as those in the Forbidden City, their elegance shows the solemnity of the imperial couple. (Courtesy of the Shenyang Imperial Palace Museum)

## Palace of Purity and Tranquility

Originally named the Middle Palace it was the residence of Huangtaiji and his empress. Located at the northern end of the Middle Section it stands with the four auxiliary palaces to its east and west and the Phoenix Tower to its south on a high terrace, forming a raised and enclosed courtyard. Five bays in width and eleven purlins in depth, it has a plain gabled roof with verandahs in front and in back. The roof is covered with yellow tiles and edged with green ones. The entrance is not in the centre but at the second bay to the east. Two flights of steps run up the platform of the building, one in the middle and the other to the east, where the entrance is. In front of the palace there is a sacrificial pole of the Manchus with a tin container at the top to hold grains and meat for crows.

**Pavilion of Respecting Ancestors** / left

The pavilion was built in the 10th year of Qianlong's reign along with the other buildings in the East and West Lodges. The pavilion was where the emperor lived when he paid a visit to Shenyang, although the original purpose of the pavilion was to house the genealogical records of the imperial family. Like other halls in the Imperial Palace in Shenyang, it has a double-eaved gable-and-hipped roof covered with yellow glazed tiles and edged with green ones and is decorated with bracket sets under the eaves. Its exterior wood members are painted with xuanzi decorative paintings. The decoration on the gables differ from those in the Forbidden City in that there is a chrysanthemum-and-ribbon design. Three running dragons decorate both sides of the main ridge, which has a flaming pearl in the centre.

**Yihe Hall** / right

The Yihe Hall was where the empress dowager stayed when the emperor traveled to Shenyang. It is in the centre of the second courtyard of the East Lodge. A three-bay-wide structure with a gable-and-hipped roof of yellow glazed tiles edged with green ones, it has verandahs at the front and at the back. The bracket sets are typical of those in the middle period of the Qing Dynasty. A door at either side opens to the courtyard in the back for eunuchs, palace maids, and servants, while the emperor and the empress dowager used the entrance in the centre. In front of the hall, bronze incense burners stand on both sides and dainty and exquisite Taihu rocks decorate the courtyard as is commonly done in gardens.

## Interior of the Yihe Hall

Partitioning screens with large opening in the centre and screen panels, with or without paintings or calligraphy, as well as classical furnishings, are often used in main halls in the Imperial Palace in Shenyang to divide the spacious halls into smaller spaces of varied sizes and to break the monotony of traditional single-storied buildings. The openwork partition embellished with jade is elegant and luxurious. The carved screen, lamps, and mirror are elaborate. The throne was used by Qianlong during his trip here. The west chamber has a couplet in Qianlong's calligraphy wishing his mother a long, happy life. The hall is calm and tranquil with the solemnity of the royal household. (Photograph by Zhao Hongsheng)

## Interior of the Jiezhi Palace / left

The Jiezhi Palace is located in the centre of the third courtyard of the East Lodge. It was where Qianlong's mother lived when she made a trip to Shenyang along with her son. It is a five-bay-wide structure with a plain gabled roof and verandahs in the front and in the back. Wood members under the eaves are painted with large-gold-spot paintings with dragon-brocade fang xin. Bracket sets without protruding tiers are placed right on the lintels. In front of the palace are rockeries and a bronze deer-shaped incense burner. Like the interior of Yihe Palace, the rooms here are divided by partitioning screens embellished with jade with large opening in the centre to create a change of space. The bedroom is in the east, the three bays in the middle are an open hall, and the west end bay is furnished with a bed and some stools. This palace was where the empress dowager rested and received the emperor for his morning greetings. (Courtesy of the Shenyang Imperial Palace Museum)

## Interior Furnishings in the Jisi Study / right

The study has a three-bay square plan divided into nine rooms of the same size with round doors leading from one to the other, giving the impression of a maze. Each room is furnished either with beds and draperies, Buddhist pictures with a table beneath, or books and scrolls-quite different from the usual decorations of court life. Jin Liang, curator of the former Museum of the Three Eastern Provinces, wrote, "The square building, a mere five zhang in width and depth, is divided into nine rooms. The emperor slept in the central room, which was surrounded by the rooms of his empress and imperial concubines. Lattice partitioning pasted with paper serves as walls. The rooms are quite secluded and sound-proof." This ingenious construction is on a par with that of the Palace of Purity and Tranquility. (Photograph by Lou Qingxi)

**Jisi Study** / upper

The study has a unique roof, of a kind not seen either in the Forbidden City or anywhere else in the Imperial Palace of Shenyang. It consists of three adjacent gabled roofs placed one behind another, forming a continuous span construction, each roof having a round ridge with overhangs on either side. The structure is three bays in width and in depth. Xuanzi decorative paintings are applied to the members under eaves. A corridor in the south of the central bay is connected to the north entrance to the Palace of Preserving Supremacy. The picture shows the Jisi Study in the foreground and the Chongmo Pavilion in the back.

**Palace of Preserving Supremacy** / lower

Located in the West Lodge of the Middle Section behind the Diguang Hall and in front of the Jisi Study, this palace was where the emperor lived when he made an inspection tour to Shenyang. In front of the palace is a small and exquisite courtyard with corridors on either side connecting the palace to the back of Diguang Hall, and the courtyard also has brick paths leading to the Di guang Hall. The palace has a plain gabled roof covered with yellow glazed tiles and edged with green ones. Running dragons decorate the main ridge and slanting ridges atop the gables. The lintels under the eaves are decorated with gilded-dragon hexi paintings. The palace is five bays wide with vermilion columns at the front and at the back, and the corbels under the lintels have designs of clouds. Rockeries and bronze vats placed on either side in front of the palace enrich and enliven the scenery and highlight the elegant tranquility of the courtyard.

## Chongmo Pavilion

Located north of Jisi Study, the pavilion stands at the northern end of the West Lodge. The architectural form and style are similar to those of the Pavilion of Respecting Ancestors. Three bays in width and depth, it is a two-storied building with a double-eaved gable-and-hipped roof. The pavilion is surrounded by corridors. The eaves are supported by bracket sets and the wood-framed members are decorated with gold-dragon hexi paintings, which show the importance of the pavilion. The plaques are inscribed in the style popular before the Qing Dynasty crossed the Great Wall and entered North China—with the Manchurian characters on the left and the Han characters on the right, just the opposite of those in the Forbidden City. A passageway in the centre runs through the first story of the pavilion. Cabinets in the pavilion contains imperial decrees and the ancient Manchurian files. There is a path for night watchmen in the high terrace courtyard to the left of the pavilion.

## Ten-prince Pavilions

The Ten-Prince Pavilions flank both sides of the Dazheng Hall and were built during Nurhachi's time together with the hall itself. The two pavilions nearest to the hall standing close to each other are the pavilions for the princes of the Left and Right Wings. The remaining eight pavilions fan out in a swallow-tail manner in the order of the Eight Banners and are also called the Eight Banner pavilions. The harmonious and unique layout of the hall and the pavilions shows an air of solemnity. In these buildings Nurhachi discussed state affairs with the banner leaders. This building complex shows the influence of the Eight Banner system on architecture in the early Qing period and is unprecedented in the history of Chinese palace architecture.

## A Corner of Eaves of the Ten-prince Pavilions

The Ten-Prince Pavilions line both sides of an imperial path leading to the Dazheng Hall. The pavilions with overhanging eaves each have a square plan, and their walls are of brick on three sides. The front sides are installed entirely with wooden latticed partition doors. The corner columns are round while those in between are octagonal. The pavilions are all topped with round-ridged gable-and-hipped roof covered with grey tiles. Beneath the eave-purlins, there are double layers of lintels connecting the upper parts of the peripteral columns with lotus-shaped blocks in between. The bracket sets are placed only on the tops of the columns.. The darkish-red wood frames under the eaves have no paintings except the brackets, corbels and the corner beams which are decorated with hoop-end paintings.

## A Corner Set of Brackets of the Dazheng Hall / left

The eaves of the octagonal hall are supported by 24 round peripteral columns one on each corner and two on each side. The lintels as tie-beams tying the tops of columns support a layer of bracket sets which protrude two tiers with double ang, similar to those of the buildings of the Han south of the Great Wall, but bigger and spaced wider apart, having only two sets of intermediate brackets placed on each lintel, i.e. between two columns. The ang are all in the shape of elephant trunks with double ang protruding outward and single one inward. Three layers of ang stick out from the corner sets of brackets placed on the corner columns to support the corner beams above. The ends of the double layers of rafters seen under the eaves are decorated with designs of swastikas or of the Chinese character for longevity. The gully-head tiles are not the ordinary kind, but resemble heart-shaped drip tiles in the lower part. This is one of the characteristics of eave tiles of the early Qing Dynasty.

## Decoration of Column Capitals of the Dazheng Hall / right

One of the earliest buildings in the Imperial Palace in Shenyang constructed between the periods of Nurhachi and Huangtaiji, the hall has a rich Manchurian and Mongolian architectural style, with features such as decorating the peripteral column capitals, a common feature of Lamaist architecture. All peripteral column capitals of the hall are covered with carved animal heads amid scroll designs. The animal heads have the face of a lion and the horns of a goat. On both sides, human hands hold whirled plants.

## Dazheng Hall

The hall is a grand palatial building. Octagonal in plan with double-eaved pyramidal roof, it is located at the prominent northern end of the East Section. During Nurhachi's time, the hall was the site of grand ceremonies such as the enthroning of an emperor, the issuing of commands for military moves, orders of general amnesty, the reception of victorious commanders and officers and royal feasts. In front of the main entrance are two columns decorated with gilded dragons, their heads raised and one front claw reaching out and the other resting on the lintel to play with a pearl. Their bodies are coiled around the columns and their tails and hind claws grip the columns. The building's eight sloping ridges are decorated with glazed sculptures of Mongol warriors.

## Imperial Throne in the Dazheng Hall

The Dazheng Hall has an imperial throne because this hall was the place where the emperor handled affairs of state in the early Qing period. The lower part of the throne is carved with two dragons frolicking with a pearl. The back of the throne is also carved with dragons. The one in the centre raises its head high, and the two on either side are curling up two posts. There are also two running dragons and two descending dragons at the end, each being lively, ferocious, and lifelike. Behind the throne is a seven-paneled screen covered with ascending and descending dragons. Nine running dragons decorate the top of the screen. The many dragons in the hall show the influence of the Han, which symbolized the omnipotent power of the emperor with dragons.

## Caisson with Descending Dragon Design in the Dazheng Hall

The octagonal caisson in the hall is supported by eight columns. Two layers of brackets laid one above the other and two rings of ornaments encircle the round centre which has a gilded carving of a dragon coiled amid floating clouds. The eight trapezoid coffers around the first layer of brackets are decorated with round lotus petals, each with a different Sanskrit character in the centre representing the four sides and eight directions shows an influence of Lamaism. The dragon in the centre of the caisson looking down ferociously from the top of layers of protruding brackets indicates royal power.

## Ceiling and Inscribed Board in the Dazheng Hall

The hall was the place where Nurhachi discussed government affairs with his ministers. Although the political centre was moved to the Chongzheng Hall after Huangtaiji, the Dazheng Hall still held an important political position. After the Qing emperors crossed the Great Wall, the hall was still the site for ceremonies and feasts when they traveled here. The picture shows a lacquered board in the hall inscribed with gilded calligraphy by Emperor Qianlong. The characters mean "Enjoy peaceful good luck." The hall is an amalgamation of Han, Manchu, Mongolian and Tibetan architecture in form, colour, decoration and construction.

## Pavilion of Literary Reminiscence

One of the principal buildings of the West Section of the Imperial Palace in Shenyang, the pavilion was built in 1781. It is one of seven such buildings that house the Complete Collection in Four Treasuries (Si Ku Quan Shu), a huge encyclopedic collection of ancient and contemporary works compiled between 1773 and 1781. Six bays (including the west end bay for staircase) wide and three bays deep, the structure has verandahs in front and in back on the first floor, giving it a steady appearance. The exterior paintings are all in Suzhou-style, and the column heads, the central parts, bottoms and ends of the lintels are decorated in red and blue. The columns are painted green, and the doors and windows are black, green, and white. The colour scheme is beautiful and elegant.

## Stone-tablet Pavilion to the East of the Pavilion of Literary Reminiscence

The Stone-Tablet Pavilion is an auxiliary structure standing to the east of the Pavilion of Literary Reminiscence. It has a square plan and a helmet-shaped roof covered with yellow glazed tiles with upturned ridge ends. The sloping ridges have no ornaments, neither animals, legendary figures, nor anything else. This style is rarely seen in other parts of China. Double-tiered bracket sets with single-qiao and single-ang are used under the eaves. The lintels on the north and south are each decorated with two gilded dragons frolicking with a pearl, and those on the east and west are embellished with paintings resembling Song tapestry. A stone tablet stands in the centre of the pavilion. On the tablet are inscribed two articles by Emperor Qianlong. On the Pavilion of Literary Reminiscence is inscribed on the front, and On Emperor Xiaozong of the Song is inscribed on the back. Both are carved in the Manchurian and Chinese languages.

## Interior of the Pavilion of Literary Reminiscence

A mezzanine floor was added to the east, west and north sides of the ground floor of the pavilion. The east and west ends of the mezzanine floor are each one bay wide. Wooden balustrades are erected along the outer sides of the mezzanine. The lattice work of the balustrades are carved with a bat design. Four panels of lattice windows are erected on two sides and are topped by a latticework with a horizontal screen. These lattice works form something like a lattice partition with draperies hung between them. The bookcases lining the north wall are covered by draperies. Boards inscribed with Qianlong's calligraphy hang in the hall, which is furnished with a throne, a desk, and an incense table. Each floor has bookcases holding the Complete Collection in Four Treasuries and the Synthesis of Past and Present Books with Illustrations. (Photograph by Lou Qingxi)

## Side Entrance to the Pavilion of Literary Reminiscence

Cold colours are used for the pavilion because it is a library. The roof is covered with black glazed tiles and edged with green ones. The main ridge is decorated with a glazed pattern of sea water and floating clouds indicating that water is pouring down from the skies to extinguish any fires. The exterior paintings are in Suzhou-style, whose themes conform to the function of the pavilion. The colours of the paintings are mainly blue, green, and white. Arched openings at the gable walls, crowned with a hanging-flower canopy of green tiles over four steps, are constructed as the entrances to the verandah of the ground floor. The boards inserted in between the bracket sets under the eaves are painted with blue dragons on a background of red. Both ends of the lintels are painted with ancient books. The limited content of these paintings shows the taste of this library.

## Illustrations of Structural Elements, Decorative and Ornamental Objects

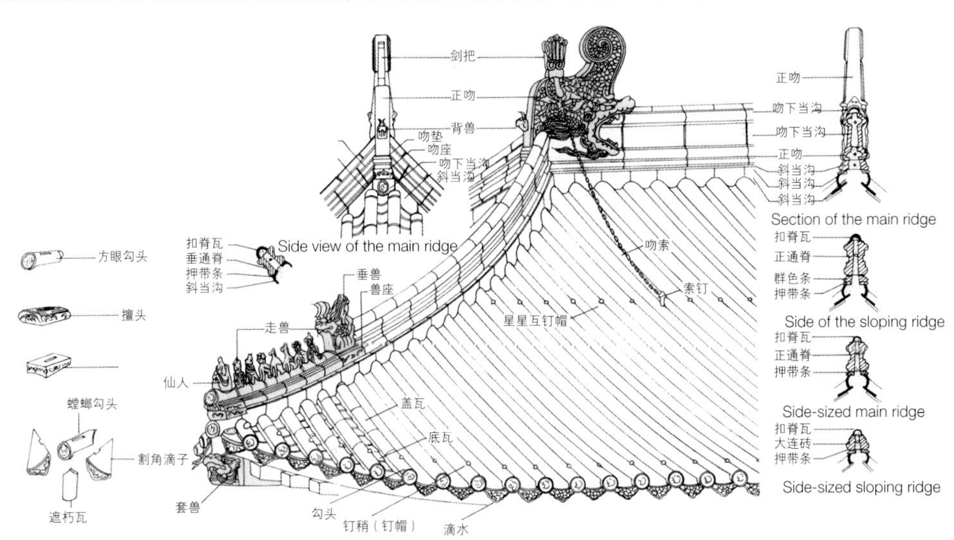


## Roofing with Glazed Tiles on Hipped Roofs

Hipped roofs, the most ancient roof form of Chinese architecture, represent the most distinguished roof form of the ancient Chinese buildings, especially roofs with double eaves, such as those of the Meridian Gate, the Hall of Supreme Harmony, the Palace of Heavenly Purity, the Palace of Earthly Tranquility, etc. A hipped roof has four slopes which form the main ridge and four sloping ridges (or hips).

Glazed tiles were used as ornamental materials for palace halls. Most palace halls used glazed tiles for roofs during the Ming and Qing dynasties. The tiles come in a variety of colours, including yellow, green, peacock blue, purple and black, with yellow being the most magnificent and green used as the secondary colour.

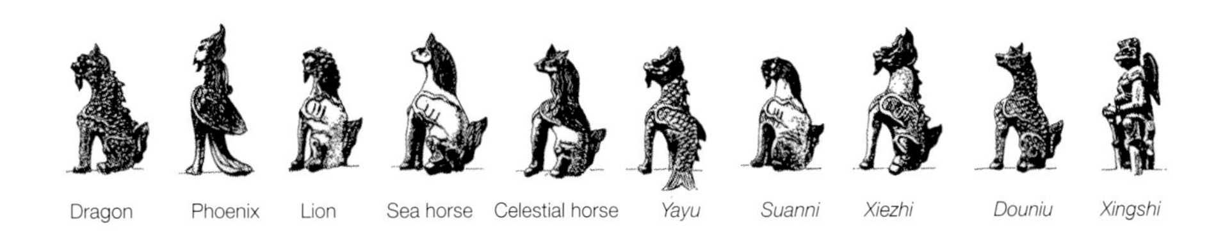


## Beast Ornaments on Ridges

A series of beast ornaments, or mythological figures, sit behind the celestial-being with the number of ornaments determined by the rank of a building. While most series have less than ten ornaments, usually in odd numbers, 10 pieces found on the Hall of Supreme Harmony in the Forbidden City indicate the highest rank of ornamentation. A series of beast ornaments, which imply luck and auspiciousness, are shown above.

## Evolution of Main Ridge Finials

In ancient times, the two ends of main ridges were fashioned with simple upturning shapes which gradually developed into finials in the shapes of animals.

The Main Hall of Foguang Temple in Mt. Wutai, Shanxi Province, features owl-tail ridge finials, with the upturned section like the back fin of a fish, and also like the upturned tail of a bird of prey. Owl-tail finials gradually gave way to owl-beak finials in the middle and late periods of the Tang Dynasty. Since the Song Dynasty dragon-shaped finials replaced owl shaped ones. They were most often used on main ridges after the Jin (Jurchen) and Yuan dynasties, and gained increasing popularity in the Ming and Qing dynasties.

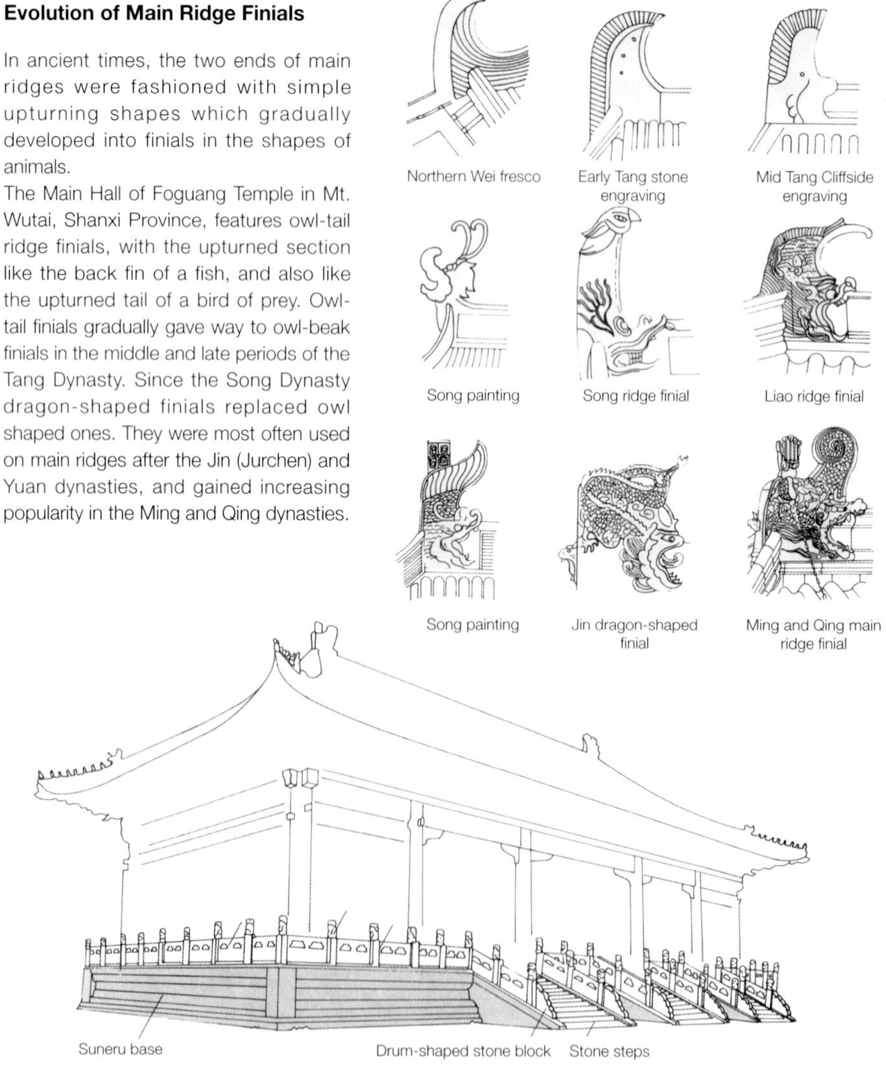


## Sumeru Bases

Diagram of a Sumeru Base

Traditional Chinese wood-framed buildings mainly consist of three parts: roofs, columns and beams, and platforms. The most typical platforms are Sumeru bases, which are mostly used as platforms of the halls in palaces and temples. Sumeru bases are normally made of bricks or stones with concave and convex moulds and carved decorative patterns. Some also have stone balustrades with upright stone posts in between. Projected dragon-head gargoyles are sometimes found under the posts.

**Song-style Sumeru base**

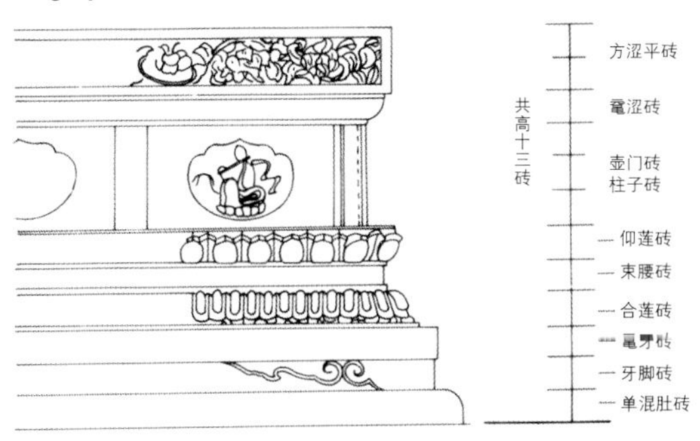


**Qing-style Sumeru base**

**Balustrade on Song-style Sumeru base**

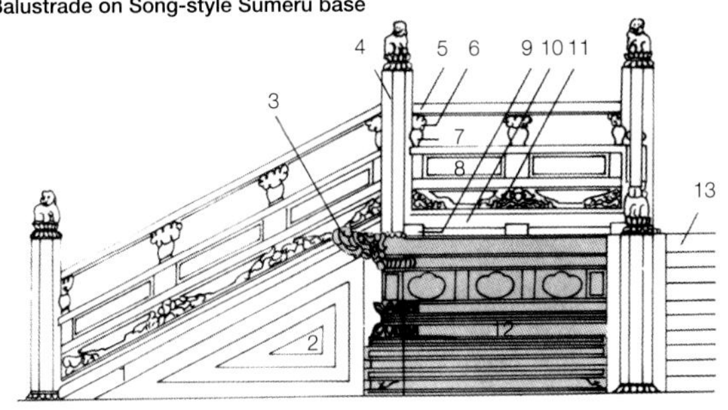


1. 副子
2. 象眼
3. 螭首
4. 望柱
5. 寻杖
6. 云
7. 瘿项
8. 花板
9. 螭子石
10. 地栿
11. 地霞
12. 须弥座
13. 踏道

**Balustrade on Qing-style Sumeru base**

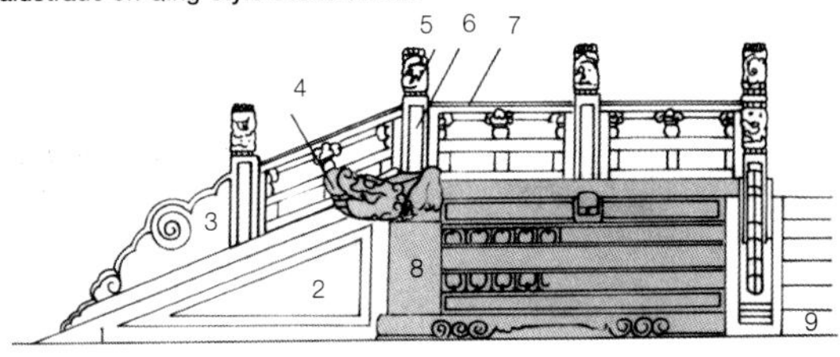


1. 垂带石
2. 象眼石
3. 抱鼓
4. 螭头
5. 柱头
6. 柱子
7. 栏板
8. 角柱
9. 踏跺

### Roof Forms of Palace Halls

The roof forms of ancient Chinese buildings offer many unique features. Building roofs are ranked in sequence: hipped roof, gable-and-hipped roof, gabled roof with overhangs and gabled roof without overhangs. The most important roofs have double layers of eaves. Besides, there are other forms including round-ridged, pinnacled (pyramidal and conical) and truncated roofs. The various roof forms feature unique corresponding structural systems. The outlines of the roofs and accompanying ridge ornaments add a sense of mystery.

The solemn and elegant roofs of the palace halls are much larger and higher than those of folk buildings. The Three Great Halls in the Forbidden City feature three roof styles — a hipped roof with double eaves, a pyramidal roof and a gable-and-hipped roof with double eaves.

Gable-and-hipped roof with double eaves

Gabled roof

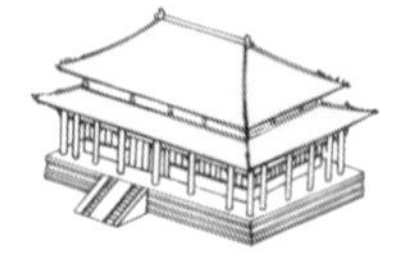

Hipped roof with double eaves

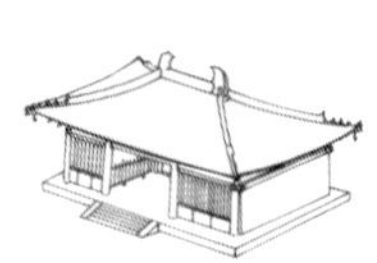

Hipped roof

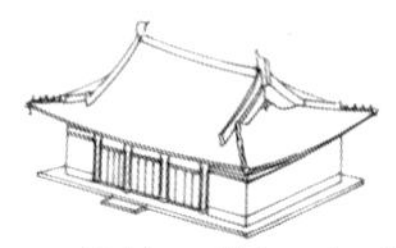

Gable-and-hipped roof

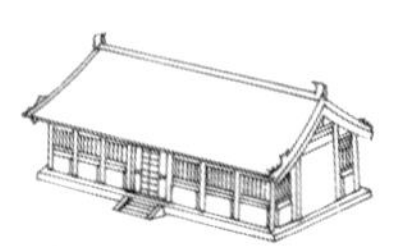

Gabled roof with overhangs

Round-ridged gable-and-hipped roof

Round-ridged gabled roof with overhangs

Round-ridged gable-and-hipped roof

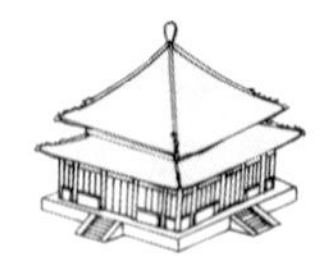

Pyramidal roof with double eaves

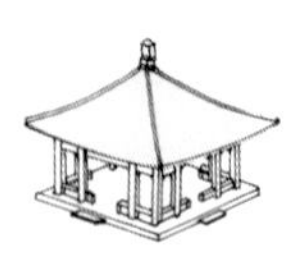

Pyramidal roof

Conical roof with double eaves

Conical roof

Octagonal pinnacled roof with double eaves

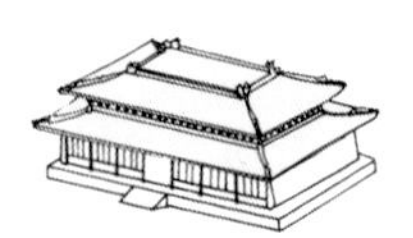

Truncated hipped roof with double eaves

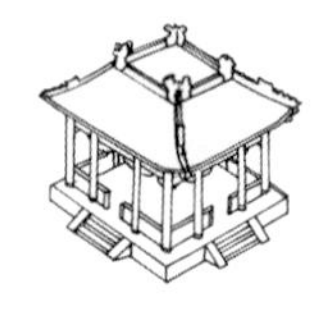

Truncated hipped roof

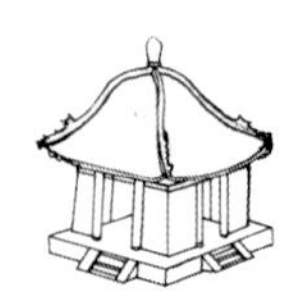

Helmet-shaped roof

## Architectural Details in Various Dynasties

| | Han | Northern and Southern Dynasties | Sui & Tang | Song, Liao & Jin | Yuan, Ming & Qing |
|---|---|---|---|---|---|
| Roof ridge ornaments | 高颐阙屋脊<br>明器屋脊<br>两城山石刻屋脊<br>两城山石刻屋脊 | 歇山顶<br>用鸱尾，屋脊曲线升起<br>河南洛阳古阳洞<br>庑殿顶<br>屋脊曲线升起<br>河南洛阳古阳洞 | 鸱尾<br>屋檐平直，<br>屋顶有鸱尾<br>西安大雁塔<br>门楣<br>版瓦屋脊及昴歇山做法 | 吻<br>泰宁甘露庵<br>吻<br>蓟县独乐寺山门 | 正吻<br>兽头<br>仙人<br>龙<br>凤 |
| Doors & Windows | 直棂窗<br>徐州汉墓<br>锁纹窗<br>徐州汉墓<br>木门<br>四川彭县画像砖<br>版门<br>徐州沛县汉墓 | 版门、直棂窗<br>河南洛阳出土北魏宁懋石室 | 破子棂窗<br>登封会善寺净芷禅师墓塔<br>直棂格子门<br>唐李思训《江帆楼阁图》 | 格子门<br>涿县普寿寺塔<br>栏槛勾窗<br>宋书雪齐江行图 | 盘长<br>套方<br>灯笼框<br>布补锦 |
| Balustrades | 斗子蜀柱栏杆<br>两城山石刻<br>栏杆<br>汉明器<br>栏杆<br>汉明器 | 直棂和勾片栏杆间用<br>甘肃敦煌莫高窟257窟<br>勾片栏杆<br>山西大同云冈9窟 | 卧棂栏杆<br>城楼基座有斗栱<br>敦煌石窟217窟<br>斗子蜀柱勾片栏杆<br>敦煌石窟25窟 | 大同下华严寺<br>易县千佛塔 | 寻杖栏杆<br>花阳杆<br>石栏杆 |
| Columns and column bases | 圆柱<br>山东安丘汉墓<br>八角柱<br>山东沂南画像石墓<br>八角柱<br>四川彭山崖墓 | 覆盆柱础<br>甘肃天水麦积山43窟<br>圆形棱柱<br>河北定兴石柱<br>八角柱<br>麦积山30窟 | 莲花柱础<br>五台山佛光寺大殿<br>莲花柱础<br>覆盆柱础<br>西安大雁塔门楣 | 盆唇覆盆柱础<br>苏州玄妙观<br>合莲卷草重层柱础<br>曲阳八会寺 | 方柱<br>圆柱<br>八角三层柱础 |
| Platforms | 台基<br>山东两城山石刻<br>台基<br>四川彭县画像砖 | 台基和砖铺散水<br>河南洛阳出土北魏宁懋石室 | 临水砖石台基<br>敦煌石窟唐代壁画<br>唐招提寺砖木台基 | 蓟县独乐寺观音阁<br>宋书《晋文公复国图》 | 须弥座<br>台基 |

## Qing-style Decorative Paintings

Magnificent paintings, the most characteristic decoration of ancient Chinese buildings, greatly enhanced architectural expression and artistic appeal. Most building paintings seen today date to the Qing Dynasty. The Qing-style decorative paintings are generally divided into three categories in terms of patterns and motifs—hexi, xuanzi and Suzhou-style paintings, which respectively symbolize nobility, elegance and liveliness.

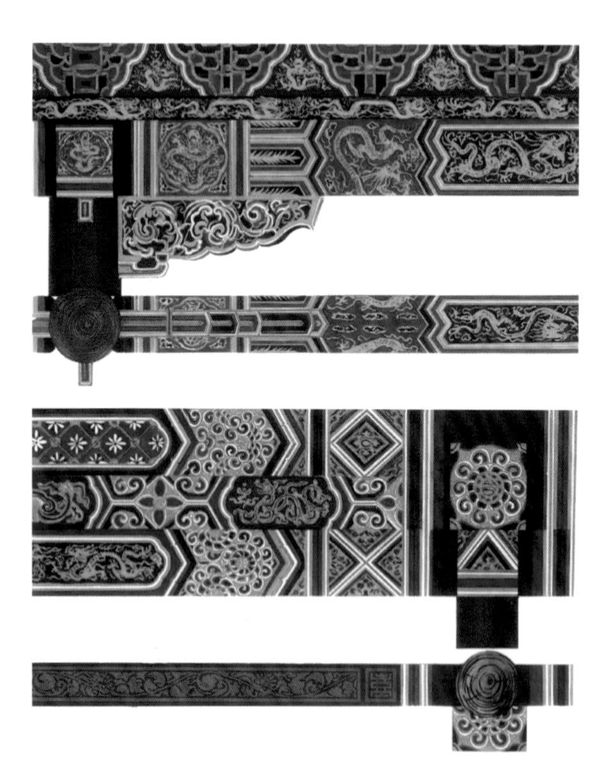

### Hexi Decorative Paintings

Hexi paintings are the highest rank, with golden-dragon patterned painting representing the highest level of nobility. Hexi paintings are most often found in important palace halls, altars or temples, e.g. the Hall of Supreme Harmony and the Hall of Prayer for Good Harvest in the Temple of Heaven, Beijing, where paintings are divided into sections by double "W"-shaped lines. Motifs of patterns on these sections are all dragons and phoenixes as well as grass. All lines and patterns are painted resplendently and magnificently with powder dribbling and gold-leafing.

### Xuanzi Decorative Painting

Xuanzi, or whirling flower, painting is named for its zao tou, or intervening section, being decorated with a motif of whirling flowers called xuanzi. The painting is divided into sections with bent lines.

Xuanzi paintings fall into seven ranks according to the amount of gold used and the application of different colours. The sequential rank includes: shinianyu with golden spots and lines, shinianyu with ink spots and lines, gold-lined with large-gold-spots, ink-lined with large-gold-spots, gold-lined with small-gold-spots, ink-lined with small-gold-spots, and yawumo (literally, elegant coloured decoration). Shinianyu (literally, flaked-jade treatment) is the most magnificent, with each petal painted with various shades of blue-green. Yawumo, the lowest ranking, uses only green, blue, black and white. Blue and green are the main colours for xuanzi paintings, with black, white and gold used for embellishment.

## Hexi Painting on Beam or Lintel with Golden-Dragon Patterns

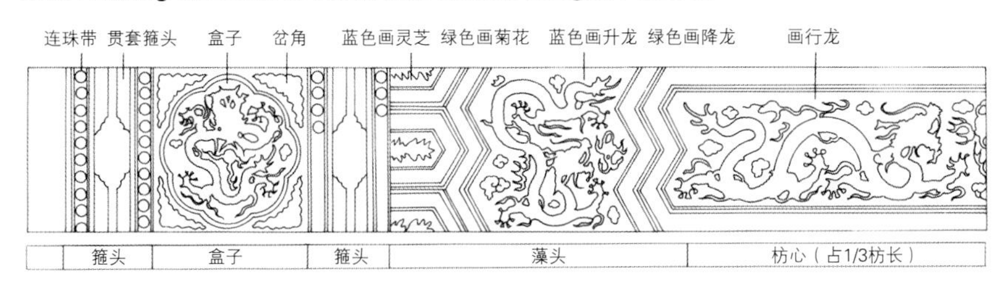


Descending dragon

Ascending dragon

Sitting dragon

Running dragon

## Hexi Painting with Golden-Dragon Patterns

Dragon patterns, as the main motifs of hexi paintings, include the golden-dragon hexi, dragon-and-phoenix hexi and dragon-and-grass hexi. Magnificent golden-dragon hexi paintings, which feature the largest amount of powder dribbling and gold-leafing, represent the highest level of nobility.

All sections of golden-dragon hexi paintings have various patterns of dragons. Generally speaking, fang xin, or the central section of a beam or lintel, features a pair of running dragons facing each other on either side of a ball. Sitting dragons are found on the two hoop ends, or gu tou, of the beam or lintel, with an ascending dragon (painted on blue background representing heaven) or a descending dragon (painted on green background representing water) on either of the intervening parts, or zao tou.

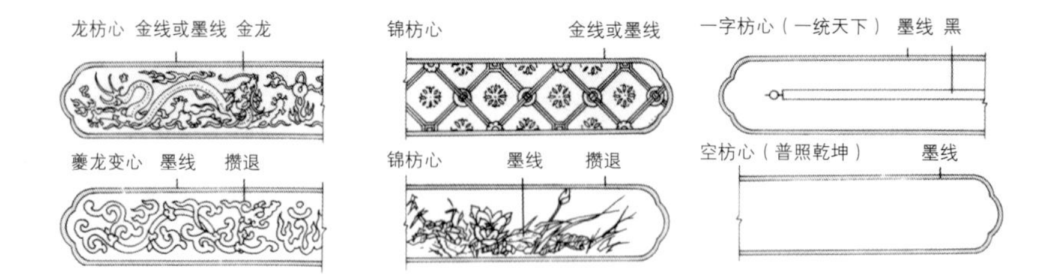


## Fang Xin of Xuanzi Decorative Paintings

Fang xin, or the central parts, or sections, of xuanzi paintings feature patterns of dragons, brocades, passion flowers, or single black lines. The pattern of a single black line is called the single-stroke fang xin. Dragons and brocades are the main subject matter of the central part, called dragon-brocade fang xin. When the fang xin of the upper lintel is painted with a dragon pattern, that of the lower lintel should be painted with a brocade one.

Dragon-brocade patterns are used for fang xin of shinianyu and gold-lined with large-gold-spots. The fang xin of ink-lined with large-gold-spots may have dragon-brocade or single-stroke pattern, or only a plain colour. The fang xin of the rest usually have plain colour patterns, kui dragons (geometric patterns of dragons), passion flowers, or other plants.

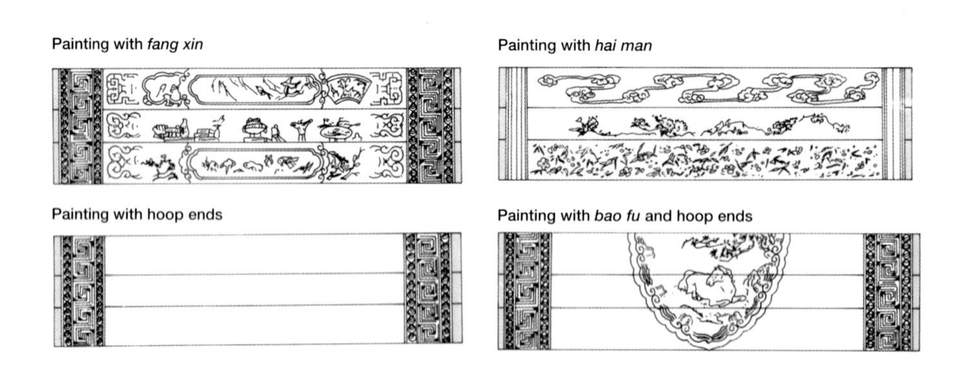
Painting with *fang xin*

Painting with *hai man*

Painting with hoop ends

Painting with *bao fu* and hoop ends

## Suzhou-style Decorative Paintings

Suzhou-style, or Su-style paintings, which were derived from southern style paintings, often feature garden buildings, houses, pavilions and corridors. The style offers a free and flexible choice of wide-ranging subjects, including flowers, fruit, celestial beings, animals, fish, birds, insects and auspicious patterns.

The sequential grades of Suzhou-style paintings include: gold-spot-and-lined, gold-lined, and yellow-lined (or ink-lined) paintings. Differences exist in the composition of the paintings, mainly in the designs of the central parts. According to the types of composition, Suzhou-style paintings may be divided into five categories: baofu (literally, wrapper), fang xin, hoop ends, hai man (literally, all-in-one), and baofu with hoop ends. Among the five, baofu, or wrapper, is the most popular.

Paintings with baofu patterns are generally applied to three adjacent wood members (usually a purlin and a lintel with a web-plate in between), where baofu is a large semi-circular panel painted in the center. Patterns of hoop ends, or gu tou, are painted at the two ends of the members. In the intervening parts, patterns of qia zi (literally, clips), ju jin (collection of choice designs), etc. are often used.

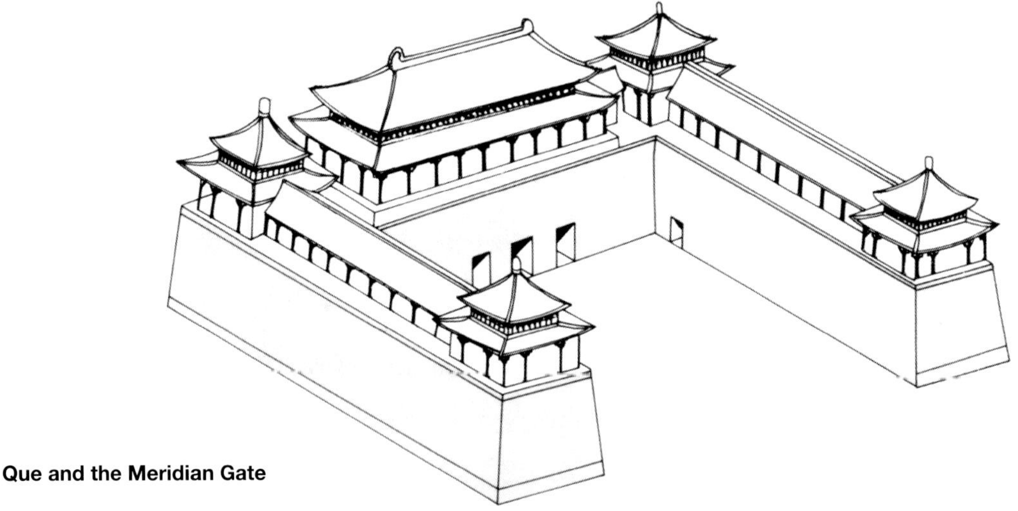

## Que and the Meridian Gate

### Meridian Gate in the Forbidden City, Beijing

The style and layout of the Meridian Gate were developed from a pair of Que according to an old saying "to show the entrance with double Que", which was also referred to as the Meridian Que or Five-Phoenix Pavilion.

In ancient China, a pair of Que was erected to demonstrate power and dignity, and sometimes it was also used as a watchtower. Gradually it was evolved into an ornamental building to show family status and social position of the occupants. The Book of Songs reflects that there have been a pair of Que since the Zhou Dynasty. During the Spring and Autumn Period Que was built at the front entrances to the palaces. In the Han Dynasty, Que was also constructed in front of palaces and mausoleums, as well as ancestral temples and tombs. There are two types of Que. One is a pair of independent Que without gate building in between, each covered with either single or double eaves. Use of this particular style of Que at tombs was limited in the Tang and Song dynasties. The other is a pair of Que separated by a gate building with gate tower featured either single, double or triple eaves. A fresco dating to the Northern Wei Dynasty shows a three-storied gate tower built on the palatial city wall in front of a palace, with left and right watch towers linked southward to the pair of Que by walls, forming a U-shaped plan. This arrangement was also adopted in the Sui and Tang dynasties. Que developed through many dynasties were shaped like the Meridian Gate in the Forbidden City.

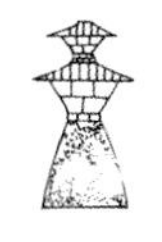

Han engraved brick

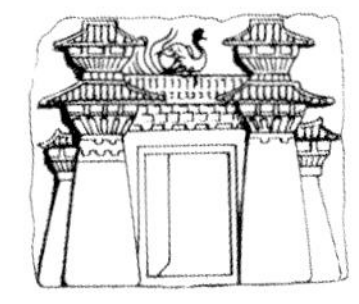

Han engraved brick

Tang stone carving

Han cliff tomb Que

Han Que

Northern Wei Que

Northern Wei Que

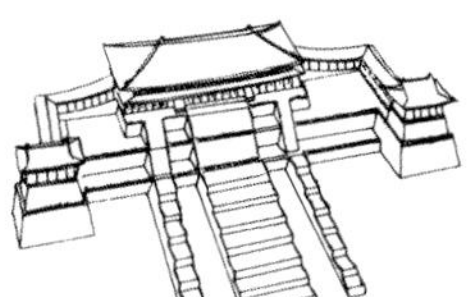

Tang palace Que

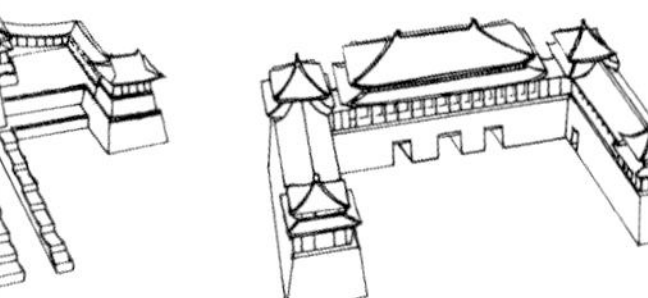

The Meridian Gate

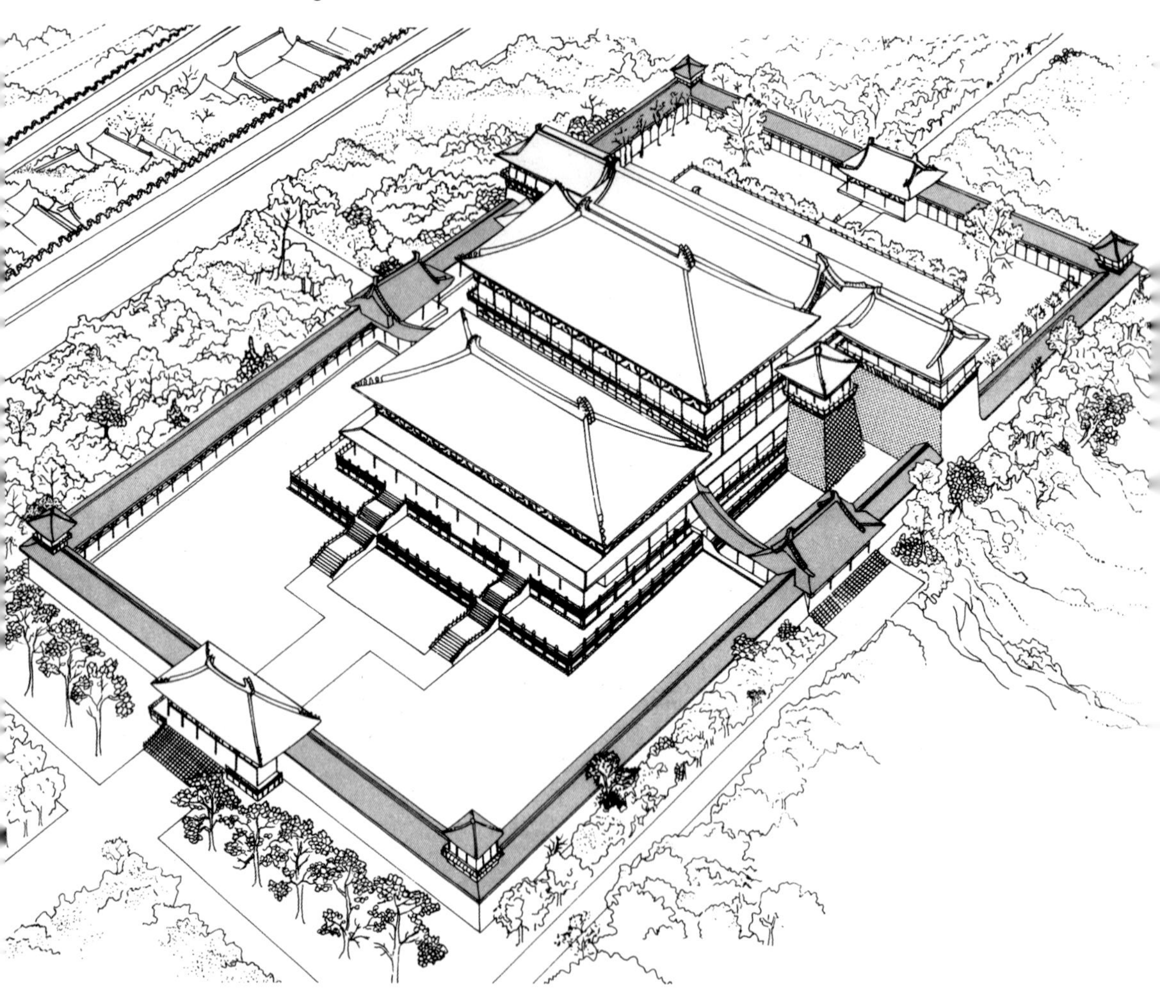

## Restoration Drawing of Linde Hall in the Tang Dynasty Daming Palace

The picture shows a restoration drawing of the Linde Hall in the Tang Dynasty Daming Palace. The Tang Dynasty emperors used the hall as a venue for entertaining officials, viewing performances and performing Buddhist rites. The hall, which sits on a mound in the northwestern section of the Palace, consists of front, central (main) and rear halls. Linde Hall is eleven bays in width and has floor space three times that of the Hall of the Supreme Harmony in the Forbidden City. A corridor, side towers and pavilions highlight the central hall.

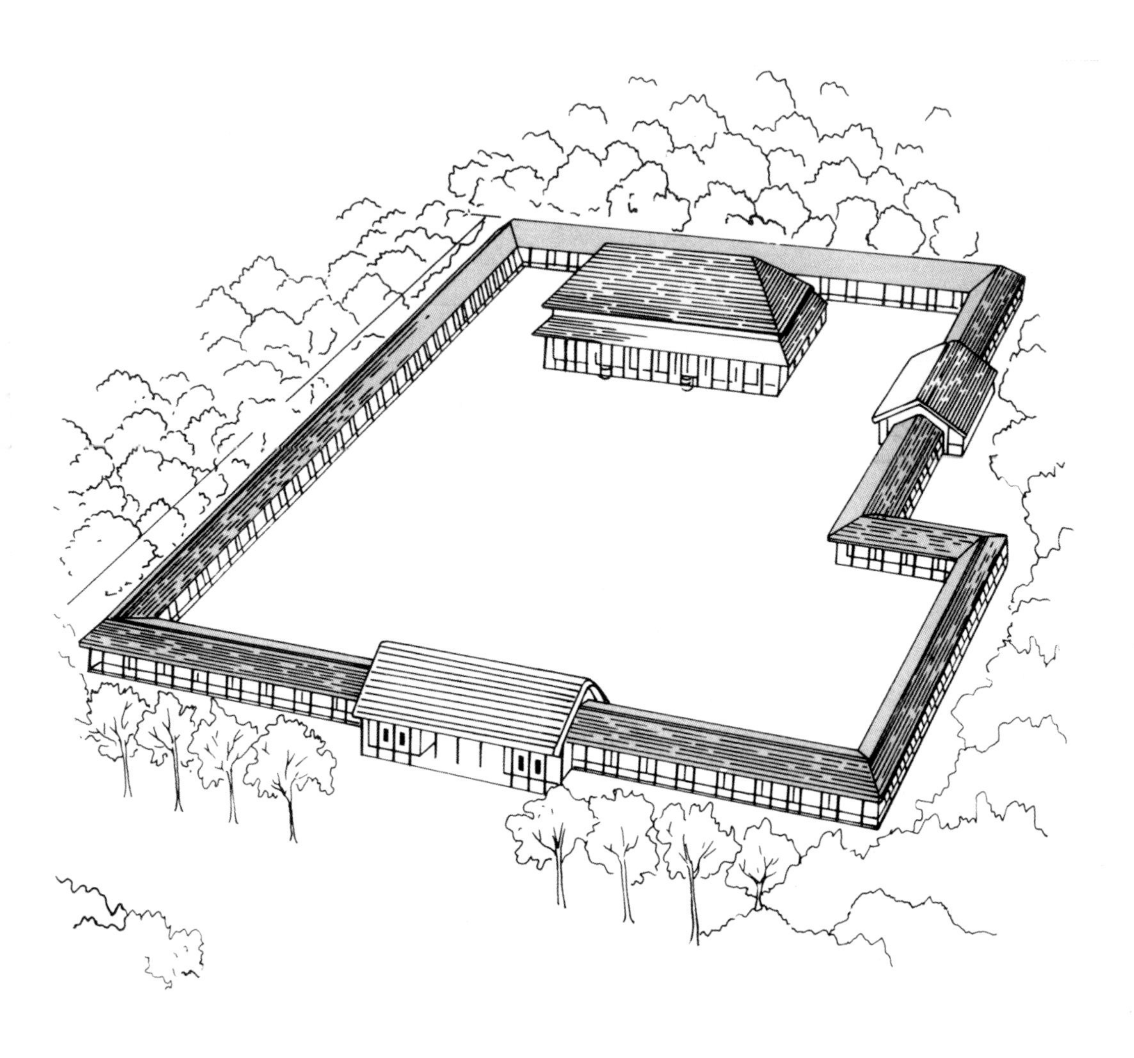

**Site of Erlitou Palace**

The ruins of Erlitou Palace, the oldest complex discovered to date, basically consist of a gate, hall and corridor. The palace ruins sit on a rammed earth terrace. The southern section of the corridor is linked to the main gate. The gate and corridor enclose a courtyard, in which a wooden hall facing south was situated at the north.

# Glossary

**ang**
a basic member projecting outward and downward like a bird's beak in a set of brackets.

**beam**
a horizontal wood member of roof-frames so installed as to support the load from purlins above and to transmit it to short posts or columns below.

**dougong or tou-kung**
bracket sets placed in a layer mainly under the eaves beyond the peristyle columns to make the eaves overhangs as far out as possible to protect wood members from the weather.

**zaojing**
caisson, a dome-like wood structure built in the ceiling of the most important hall, below which an imperial throne or a Buddhist statue was usually situated.

**coffered ceiling**
a kind of ceilings usually installed in palatial halls which is constructed with joists placed crisscross, forming a uniformly squared grid with painted ceiling boards inserted in each of the squares.

**cross-ridge**
a ridge on the top of a roof formed by two horizontal ridges intersecting as a cross in plan.

**decorative painting**
traditional polychrome painting on wood members.

**dou**
basic members in a set of brackets with the shape of wooden blocks. There are two kinds of such blocks, a main block placed at the foot of the bracket set and a number of secondary blocks placed in between the other members.

**efang**
a lintel, or a horizontal member, connecting tops of peristyle columns, on which a plate supporting intermediate sets of brackets is placed. Two lintels, an upper one and a lower one with a plate (web piece ) in between, are usually used in buildings of importance.

**exterior finish work**
a kind of non-loadbearing woodwork fitted under the open eaves or separating the interior from the exterior space, such as doors, windows, decorative panels, and balustrades.

**feng-shui**
geomantic theories for location of a building complex or tombs supposed to have an influence on the fortune of the occupants, literally, wind and water.

**gable-and-hipped roof**
a hipped roof with small gables on the two sides, i.e. a roof with its upper part gabled and its lower part hipped.

**gabled roof with overhangs at its two sides**
two-sloped roof with its two sides overhung, forming a gable at each side.

**gabled roof without overhangs at its two sides**
two-sloped roof with flush ends enclosed by bricks at its two sides.

**gargoyle**
a sculptural projection in the shape of the head of a chi, hornles dragon, from a terrace scupper to drop rain water away.

**goldleafing**
a special technique of gold foil pasting with gold glue in decorative painting, closely related to the technique of powderdribbling.

**gong**
basic members of bracket sets, which are bow-shaped and parallel to the building facade. A gong is usually set on a bearing block at its centre and supports a secondary block at each upraised end.

**hall**
a building of importance, usually single-storeyed, larger in size and higher in quality, with hipped or gable-and-hipped roof, in a palace or a temple.

**hexi painting**
one of the three categories of decorative paintings in the Qing Period, which is applied to the highest ranking with patterns in dragon and phoenix motives.

**hipped roof**
a roof which has four slopes with a horizontal ridge at the top and four hips which are called " the sloping ridges" where two adjacent slopes meet. In traditional Chinese architecture, the slopes are all slightly curved and roofs of this type could only be used to cover those higher ranking buildings or the main halls in palaces or temples.

**hypostyle columns**
interior columns located on the second line next to the line of the peristyle columns.

**interior finish work**
a kind of non-loadbearing woodwork fitted in the interior space or separating the interior space, such as partitions, panelled screens, coffered ceilings, and caisson ceilings.

**jian**
a unit of space in rtaditional Chinese architecture, which is defined as the space bounded by four columns, For example, the Hall of Supreme Harmony is 11 bays in width and 5 bays in depth, so that it has 72 columns with a apace of 55 jian.

**mandala**
Sanskrit for a Buddhist shrine of Bodhisattvas.

**palace**
a palatial complex or the main hall of a palatial complex.

**partition door**
a door leaf fitted with other leaves forming a partition to divide interio space or to separate interior from exterior space. The number of door leaves is contingent on the width of the bay, usually being four, six or eight. A partition door is composed of a latticed sash on the upper part and a few panels on the lower part, framed by stiles and rails.

**pavilion**
(1) *ting*, a single-storeyed kiosk usually located in a garden;
(2) *ge*, a multi-storeyed building.

**peristyle columns**
columns located on the outer line under the eaves.

**platform**
the base of a building. In traditonal Chinese architecture, the platform is an integral part of the building it carries. It is often constructed of stone piers at the corners with brick or stone filling between the piers and stone curbs covering its upper edges. For some important buildings or hall, Sumeru bases are usually built in place of the platforms.

**powder dribbling**
a special technique of trickling powder paste to make raised lines in preparation for goldleafing on decorative painting.

**qiao**
an arm-shaped member projecting outward or inward in a set of brackets.

**queti**
a decorated corbel or bracket inserted in a peristyle column projecting out to support the lintels.

**ridge**
raised line where two sloping roof surfaces meet. In traditional Chinese architecture, a ridge may be horizontal or sloping.

**silled window**
a window leaf fitted with other leaves on the window sill of the side bay of a hall. Windows of this kind are very commonly used in palaces and temples.

**Sumeru base**
a special kind of the base of a building or a hall. It was said that Sumeru was a fabled mountain in ancient India which was the centre of the world that the sun and the moon moved around. Originally, the Sumeru base was used as a dais of the Buddha statues. Since Buddhism came to China, it became the base of a building.

**Su-style painting**
or Suzhou-style painting, one of the three categories of decorative paintings in the Qing Period, which is mainly used in imperial gardens with motives of landscapes, episodes from folk tales, flowers and birds.

**tiao**
a tier of projection outward or inward of a bracket set, literally a "jump".

**wu xing**
five elements, which are five different kinds of matter that people constantly come to contact with, i.e. wood, fire, earth, metal and water, which the Chinese ancients believed to form the physical universe with.

**xuanzi painting**
one of the three categories of decorative paintings in the Qing Period, which is immediately subordinate to hexi painting and is widely used in the secondary buildings with the motives of whirling flowers.

**yin and yang**
the ancient Chinese principles of the two elements in nature, which are mutually opposing but dependent on each other for existence. It is believed that everything in the world has two respects: yin and yang. For example, pairs of above and below, front and back; numbers in odd and even, positive and negative; sexes of masculine and feminine, are classified as follows: above, front, odd, positire and masculine belong to yang,whereas below, back, even, negative and feminine stand for yin.

# Chronology of Major Events in the History of Chinese Architecture

| Christian era | Chinese Dynastic Years | Events or Achievements |
|---|---|---|
| The Neolithic Age | | |
| ca. 4800 BC | | Sites of ganlan buildings (pile-supported structures with wooden floor above the ground) of Hemudu Culture were unearthed in the northeast of Hemudu Village in Yuyao County, Zhejiang Province. |
| ca. 4500 BC | | Sites of Various kinds of primitive houses of Yangshao Culture, including a big house square in plan were unearthed in Banpo Village near Xi'an, Shaanxi Province. |
| 2310~2378 BC | | A sacrificial altar of Liangzhu Culture was unearthed at Yaoshan in Yuhang County, Zhejiang Province. |
| ca. 3000 BC | | Temple of Goddess of Hongshan Culture was discovered at Niuheliang in Lingyuan County, Liaoning Province |
| The Shang Dynasty | | |
| 1900~1500 BC | | An Early Shang site of a high-terrace palatial complex was unearthed at Erlitou Village in Yanshi County, Henan Province. |
| 17th~11th c. BC | | Rectangular houses with rammed earth foundations and walls were unearthed in present Zhengzhou, Henan Province. |
| 1384 BC | 15th year, Pangeng | Capital of the Shang was moved to Yin where the Late Shang capital was constructed, which was unearthed and referred to as the Yin Ruins at Xiaotun Village in Anyang, Henan Province. |
| The Western Zhou Dynasty | | |
| 1095 BC | 10th year, Chengwang | An ancestral temple of the Zhou Court was unearthed at Fengchu Village in Qishan County, Shaanxi Province. |
| The Spring and Autumn Period | | |
| 475 BC | 45th year, Jingwang | Rules for capital planning of the Zhou Court were recorded in the Survey on Construction Work collected in the Ritual of Zhou, in which it was regulated that the Ancestral Temple was to be located to the left of the palace, and the Altar of Land and Grain, to its right. |
| The Warring States Period | | |
| 350~207 BC | | Site of Xianyang Palace of the Qin State, a high-terrace building complex, was unearthed at Xianyang, Shaanxi Province. |
| The Qin Dynasty | | |
| 221 BC | 26th year, Shi Huang Di | The Qin conquered the six states and built palaces in styles to imitate those of the conquered states on the northern sloping fields of Xianyang.<br>An army of 300,000 men, led by Meng Tian, was sent to drive out the northern nomadic Hun invasions and to build the Great Wall from Lintao (in present-day Gansu province) in the west to Liaodong (the east of present-day Liaoning Province) in the east.<br>Capital Xianyang was constructed and extended. |
| 221~210 BC | 26th~37th years, Shi Huang Di | Construction of Shi Huang Di's mausoleum started in Lintong, Shaanxi Province. |
| 212 BC | 35th year, Shi Huang Di | Construction of the Epang (or Efanggong) Palace began on the south bank of the Wei River, Xianyang. |
| The Western Han Dynasty | | |
| 200 BC | 7th year, Gaozu | Palatial city in Chang'an (present-day Xi'an) was under construction and Changle Palace (Palace of Everlasting Happiness) was erected. |
| 199 BC | 8th year, Gaozu | Construction of Wei Yang palace started. The Palace was completed in the next year. |
| 140~87 BC | Reign period of Wudi | Construction of Maoling Tomb (the Mausoleum of Emperor Wudi) started in Xingping County, Shaanxi Province. |
| 138 BC | 4th year, Jianyuan, Wudi | Shang Lin Garden of the Qin was extended in a vast area of 300 li across with 70 detached palaces included. |
| 127 BC | 2nd year, Yuanshuo, Wudi | The Great Wall with watchtowers, passes and beacon towers was reconstructed. Later on, the Great wall underwent five large-scale reconstruction works. |

| Christian era | Chinese Dynastic Years | Events or Achievements |
|---|---|---|
| 104 BC | 1st year, Taichu, Wudi | Jian Zhang Palace was built in the western outskirts of Chang'an City. |
| 101 BC | 4th year, Taichu, Wudi | Ming Guang Palace was built in the City of Chang'an. |
| 32 BC | 1st year, Jianshi, Chengdi | Altars for offering sacrifices to God of Heaven and God of Earth were erected in the southern and northern suburbs of Chang'an respectively. Thereafter the locations of the Altar of Heaven and the Altar of Earth in the planning of the capital city were so established as a rule. |
| 4 AD | 4th year, Yuanshi, Pingdi | Mingtang, Biyong (halls for handling state affairs and promulgating politics as well as schooling) and Lingtai (Terrace of Spirit) were erected inside and outside Chang'an. |
| **The Xin Dynasty** | | |
| 20 AD | 1st year, Dihuang, Wang Mang | More than ten palaces, including Jian Zhang Palace, were demolished. The disassembled materials were used to build eleven buildings in the southern suburbs of Chang'an, known as the Nine Temples of Wang Mang historically. |
| **The Eastern Han Dynasty** | | |
| 68 AD | 11th year, Yongping, Mingdi | Baima Si (the Temple of White Horse) was erected in Luoyang. |
| **Period of the Three Kingdoms** | | |
| 220 AD | 1st year, Huangchu, Wendi of the Wei | Cao Pi founded the Kingdom of Wei with its capital moved from Yecheng to Luoyang. |
| 221 AD | 1st year, Zhangwu, the Shu Han | Liu Bei founded the Kingdom of Shu Han, making Chengdu (in present-day Sichuan province) its capital. |
| 229 AD | 8th year, Huangwu, the Wu | Sun Quan moved the capital of the Kingdom of Wu from Wuchang to Jianye (present-day Nanjing). The capital city with the palace were then constructed. |
| 235 AD | 3rd year, Qinglong, Mingdi of the Wei | The Palace of Luoyang of the Wei Court was built at Luoyang. |
| 237 AD | 1st year, Jingchu, Mingdi of the Wei | The Garden of Fragrant Forest (Fang Lin Yuan) was completed and the Hill of Jingyang was piled up in Luoyang |
| **The Jin Dynasty** | | |
| ca. 300 AD | ca. 1st year, Yongkang, Huidi | Shi Chong built a garden at the Golden Ravine in the northeastern outskirts of Luoyang, known as the Garden of Golden Ravine. |
| 332 AD | 7th year, Xianhe, Chengdi | The Palace of Jiankang was built in Jiankang (present-day Nanjing). |
| 347 AD | 3rd year, Yonghe, Mudi | An imperial garden called Hualin Garden was built at the southern bank of Xuanwu Lake in Jiankang. About a hundred years later, the Song of the Southern Dynasties built another garden called the Pleasure Garden to the east of Hualin Garden. |
| 353~366 AD | | Mogao Grottoes at Dunhuang, in present-day Gansu Province, were first dug out. |
| 400 AD | 4th year, Long'an, Andi | Buddhist Monk Huichi built the Temple of Samantabhadra (present-day the Wannian Temple) at Mount Emei in Sichuan. |
| 413 AD | 9th year, Yixi, Andi | Helianbobo built Tongwancheng, capital city of the Great Xia Dynasty (in presentday Inner Mongolia). |
| **The Northern and Southern Dynasties** | | |
| 452~464 AD | Wenchengdi, Northern Wei | Yungang Grottoes at Datong, Shanxi, were first hollowed out. |
| 494~495 AD | 18th~19th years, Taihe, Northern Wei | Longmen Grottoes at Luoyang, Henan, were first hollowed out. |
| 513 AD | 2nd year, Yanchang, Northern Wei | Grottoes of Bingling Temple, a Buddhist cave temple in Gansu, was built. |
| 516 AD | 1st year, Xiping, Northern Wei | Wooden Pagoda of the Temple of Everlasting Tranquillity (Yongning Temple) was erected up in Luoyang. |
| 523 AD | 4th year, Zhengguang, Northern Wei | Brick Pagoda of the Songyue Temple at Dengfeng in Henan was built. |
| **The Sui Dynasty** | | |
| 582 | 2nd year, Kaihuang, Wendi | Yuwen Kai was appointed to design and construct the capital city Daxing (present-day Xi'an), which was renamed as Chang'an in the Tang Dynasty. |
| 586 | 6th year, Kaihuang, Wendi | Construction of the Longzang Buddhist Temple at Zhengding, Hebei, started. The temple was renamed as the Longxing Temple in the reign period of Emperor Kangxi of the Qing Dynasty. |
| 595 | 15th year, Kaihuang, Wendi | Palace of Benevolence and Longevity (Ren Shou Gong) was built in Daxing, capital of the Sui Dynasty. |
| 607 | 3rd year, Daye, Yangdi | One million men were sent to repair and restore the Great Wall. |
| 611 | 7th year, Daye, Yangdi | The Four-Gate Pagoda, a single-storeyed pagoda, of Shentong Temple in Licheng, Shandong, was built. |

| Christian era | Chinese Dynastic Years | Events or Achievements |
|---|---|---|
| The Tang Dynasty | | |
| 618~916 | | Double-storeyed single-sealed dwelling houses came into being, while multi-storeyed buildings became on the wane. |
| 627~648 | Period of Zhenguan, Taizong | Mount Hua in Shaanxi, one of the Five Sacred Mountains in ancient China, was granted as the Golden Heavenly King, where the Temple of Western Sacred Mountain was built. |
| 630 | 4th year, Zhenguan, Taizong | Orders were given to erect Confucian Temples in the schools of prefectures and counties all over the country. |
| 636 | 10th year, Zhenguan, Taizong | Construction of Zhaoling Tomb (the Mausoleum of Emperor Taizong) began in Liquan County, Shaanxi. |
| 651 | 2nd year, Yonghui,Gaozong | Taziks (the Arabian Empire) sent envoys to the Tang Court. Since then, the Islamic architecture came into being in China. |
| 7th century | | Huaisheng Si (literally, the Mosque in Memory of the Saint) was first built in Guangzhou, Guangdong. |
| 652 | 3rd year, Yonghui,Gaozong | The Great Wild Goose Pagoda of Ci'en Temple in Chang'an (present-day Xi'an) was built. |
| 669 | 2nd year, Zongzhang, | The Pagoda of Xuanzang was built in Xingjiao Temple in Chang'an. |
| 681 | 1st year, Kaiyao, Gaozong | The Pagoda of Xiangji Temple in Chang'an was built. |
| 683 | 1st year, Hongdao, Gaozong | Construction of Qianling Tomb (the Mausoleum of Emperor Gaozong) began in Qianxian County, Shaanxi. |
| 707~709 | 1st~3rd years, Jinglong,Zhongzong | The Small Wild Goose Pagoda of Jianfu Temple in Chang'an was built. |
| 714 | 2nd year, Kaiyuan,Xuanzong | Construction of Xingqing Palace in Chang'an started. |
| 722 | 10th year, Kaiyuan, Xuanzong | The Tianchang Taoist Temple in Youzhou (present-day Beijing) was first built. The Temple was renamed as Baiyun Guan, or the Temple of White Clouds, in the early Ming Dynasty. |
| 724 | 12th year, Kaiyuan, Xuanzong | Jianfu Palace at the foot of Qingcheng Mountain in Sichuan was first built. |
| 725 | 13th year, Kaiyuan, Xuanzong | The Huaqing Pool with a detached palace was built at Lishan in Lintong County, Shaanxi. The Qujiang Pool with a recreation garden was built in Chang'an. |
| 782 | 3rd year, Jianzhong, Dezong | The Main Hall of Nanchan Temple in Mount Wutai, Shanxi, was built. |
| 857 | 11th year, Dazhong, Xuanzong | The Eastern Hall of Foguang Temple in Mount Wutai, Shanxi, was built. |
| The Five Dynasties | | |
| 956 | 3rd year, Xiande,Shizong, Late Zhou | The Later Zhou made Kaifeng the capital, and then, extended it on the basis of the capital of the Later Liang and Later Jin. Thereafter, Kaifeng was further developed especially when it was made capital of the Northern Song Dynasty. |
| 959 | 6th year, Xiande,Shizong, Late Zhou | The Pagoda of Yunyan Temple at Suzhou, Jiangsu, was built. |
| The Northern Song and Liao (Khitan)Dynasties | | |
| 960~1279 | | Style and form of local dwelling houses were gradually finalized with less difference from those of the Qing period. |
| 964 | 2nd year, Qiande,Taizu, the Song | The Temple of Central Sacred Mountain at Songshan, Henan, was renovated. |
| 971 | 4th year, Kaibao,Taizu, the Song | The Pavilion of Buddha Fragrance (Foxiang Ge) at Longxing Temple in Zhengding, Hebei, was first built with a 24-metre-high bronze statue of Guanyin (Goddess of Mercy, or Avalokitesvara) housed in. |
| 977 | 2nd year, Taipingxingguo,Taizong, the Song | The Longhua Pagoda was erected in Shanghai. |
| 984 | 2nd year, Tonghe,Shengzong, the Liao | The Guanyin Pavilion and the Entrance Hall of Dule Temple at Jixian County in present day Tianjin were built. |
| 996 | 14th year, Tonghe,Shengzong, the Liao | Libai Si of Niujie, or the Mosque of Ox Street, in Beijing was first built. |
| 1009 | 2nd year, Dazhongxiangfu,Zhenzong, the Song | Tiankuang Dian (literally, the Hall of Godsend) of Dai Miao (Temple of Eastern Sacred Mountain) was built on the foot of Mount Tai, Shandong.<br>Temple of Princess Aurora was built on the top of Mount Tai. |
| 1009 | 2nd year, Dazhongxiangfu,Zhenzong, the Song | The Ashab Mosque at Quanzhou, Fujian, was first built. |

| Christian era | Chinese Dynastic Years | Events or Achievements |
|---|---|---|
| 1038 | 7th year, Chongxi,Xingzong, the Liao | The Bhagavat Storage Hall (Bojia Jiaozang Dian) of the Lower Huayan Temple in Datong, Shanxi, was built. |
| 1052 | 4th year, Huangyou,Renzong, the Song | The Hall of Sakyamuni (Moni Dian) of Longxing Temple in Zhengding, Hebei, was built. |
| 1056 | 2nd year, Qingning,Daozong, the Liao | The Pagoda of Sakyamuni, or the Wooden Pagoda, of Fogong Temple at Yingxian, Shanxi, was erected. |
| 1100 | 3rd year, Yuanfu,Zhezong, the Song | Li Jie finalized the book Building Standard, or treatise On Architectural Methods, which was promulgated by the Song Court in 1103 as building codes for design and construction works. |
| 1102 | 1st year, Chongning,Huizong, the Song | The Shengmu Hall, or the Hall of Sacred Mother, of Jin Ci, a memorial temple of Jin, in Taiyuan, Shanxi, was restored. |
| 1115 | 5th year, Zhenghe,Huizong, the Song | It is recorded that there were more than ten thousand workers everyday forced to build Mingtang for the emperor in Kaifeng. |
| 1125 | 7th year, Xuanhe,Huizong, the Song | The Chuzu Nunnery, or the Hall of Patriarch, of Shaolin Temple in Dengfeng, Henan, was built. |
| 12th century | | The Minaret of Light was built in Huaisheng Si, or the Mosque in Memory of the Saint, in Guangzhou, Guangdong. |
| The Southern Song and Jin (Jurchen)Dynasties | | |
| 12th century | | Han Tuozhou built his personal garden, called the Southern Garden, in Lin'an (present-day Hangzhou). Han Shizong built his personal garden, called Meigang Garden (literally, the Garden of Plum Blossom Ridge), in Lin'an. |
| 1138 | 8th year, Shaoxing,Gaozong, the Song | The Song Court moved to Lin'an where the temporary palace was arranged. Lin'an was then decided upon as the temporary capital and was extended. |
| 1150 | 2nd year, Tiande,Qingdi, the Jin | Wanyan Liang, emperor of the Jurchen (Jin), renamed Youzhou (present-day Beijing) as the Middle Capital of the Jurchen, and assigned Zhang Hao and Kong Yanzhou to the construction of the Middle Capital. |
| 1163 | 3rd year, Dading,Shizong, the Jin | The Confucian Temple with its main hall, Dacheng Dian, at Pingyao, Shanxi, was built. |
| 1240 | 12th year, Taizong of the Mongols | The Palace of Perpetual Happiness, or Yongle Gong, was built at Yongle Town in Yongji County, Shanxi. It is a Taoist temple in memory of Lu Dongbin, one of the Eight Taoist Immortals, and it was said that Yongle Town was Lu Dongbin's birthplace. |
| 1267 | 4th year, Zhiyuan,Shizu of the Mongols | The Mongol Emperor Kublai Khan moved the capital to Youzhou (present-day Beijing), and renamed it as Dadu, or the Great Capital. Liu Bingzhong was appointed to plan and construct the Great Capital. |
| 1269 | 6th year, ZhiyuanShizu of the Mongols | The Imperial College (the highest educational administration) was established in Dadu (the Great Capital). |
| 1271 | 8th year, Zhiyuan,Shizu of the Yuan | In Miaoying Temple, a Lamasery in Beijing, the White Dagoba, which is a pagoda in Lamaist style, was erected. It is the earliest dagoba preserved intact in China. |
| 1275 | 1st year, Deyou,Gongdi, the Song | Tomb of Puhading, sixteenth generation descendent of Mohammed, was built in Yangzhou, Jiangsu. Xianhe Si (literally, the Mosque of White Crane) was erected in Yangzhou. |
| The Yuan Dynasty | | |
| 13th century | Early Yuan Period | The Southern Temple of Saga in Saga County, Tibet, was built. |
| 13th century | Early Yuan Period | The Hill of Longevity and the Imperial Lake were constructed in Dadu (the Great Capital) as the Imperial Garden of the Yuan Court. The Hill of Longevity was constructed on the Jade Flower Islet (or Qionghua Island) of the Jin, which is in Beihai Park of today's Beijing. |
| 1302 | 6th year, Dade, Chengzong | The Confucian Temple in Dadu (present-day Beijing) was built. |
| 1309 | 2nd year, Zhida, Wuzong | The Ashab Mosque at Quanzhou, Fujian, was renovated. |
| 1323 | 3rd year, Zhizhi, Yingzong | Islamic Holy Tombs of Quanzhou, Fujian, were renovated. |
| 1342 | 2nd year, Zhizheng, Shundi | Tian Ru, a Buddhist abbot, built the Shizi Lin (Garden of Lion Grove) in Suzhou. |
| 1350 | 10th year, Zhizheng, Shundi | Huaisheng Si, or the Mosque in Memory of the Saint, in Guangzhou was renovated. |
| 1356 | 16th year, Zhizheng, Shundi | The Mosque of Dongsi in Beijing was first built. It was renovated in 1447. |
| 1363 | 23rd year, Zhizheng, Shundi | Mausoleum of Tuheluk Timur at Huocheng near Gulja (Yining), Xinjiang, was built. |
| The Ming Dynasty | | |
| 1368 | 1st year, Hongwu,Taizu | The Ming Court began to construct its imperial palace in Nanjing. |

| Christian era | Chinese Dynastic Years | Events or Achievements |
|---|---|---|
| 1373 | 6th year, Hongwu, Taizu | Construction of the Capital City of Nanjing as well as the imperial palace was completed.<br>General Xu Da was appointed to garrison the northern frontiers. Based on Hua Yunlong's proposal, the Great Wall was first rebuilt. It was renovated and extended several times in the Ming period.<br>Temple for Offering Sacrifices to Emperors of the Past Dynasties was built on the southern slope of Qintian Hill in Nanjing. |
| 1376~1383 | 9th~15th year, Hongwu, Tai | The Main Hall of Linggu Temple, a vaulted beamless building, in Nanjing was built. |
| 1381 | 14th year, Hongwu, Taizu | Construction of Xiaoling Tomb (the Mausoleum of Emperor Taizu) started in Nanjing. The tomb was completed in 1405. |
| 1407 | 5th year, Yongle, Chengzu | Construction of the Forbidden City in Beijing began. |
| 1409 | 7th year, Yongle, Chengzu | Construction of Changling Tomb (the Mausoleum of Emperor Yongle) began in Changping County, Beijing. |
| 1413 | 11th year, Yongle, Chengzu | An imperial order was given to build Taoist building complexes in Wudang Mountain, Hubei. It took 11 years to build up 8 palaces, 2 temples, 36 nunneries and 72 cliff temples. |
| 1420 | 18th year, Yongle, Chengzu | City of Beijing with the Imperial City and Forbidden City included was completed. Capital of the Ming moved to Beijing.<br>In Beijing, the Altar of Heaven, the Altar of Earth, the Imperial Ancestral Temple and the Altar of Agriculture were built. |
| 1421 | 19th year, Yongle, Chengzu | The Three Great Halls of the Forbidden City were destroyed by fire.<br>The Altar of Land and Grain in Beijing was built. |
| 1436 | 1st year, Zhengtong, Yingzong | The Three Great Halls of the Forbidden City were rebuilt. |
| 1442 | 7th year, Zhengtong,Yingzong | Libai Si of Niujie, or the Mosque of Ox Street, in Beijing was renovated. The Mosque was thoroughly restored and extended in 1696. |
| 1444 | 9th year, Zhengtong,Yingzong | Zhihua Temple in Beijing was built. |
| 1447 | 12th year, Zhengtong,Yingzong | Tashilunpo Monastery was built in Xigaze, Tibet. |
| 1473 | 9th year, Chenghua,Xianzong | Diamond Throne Pagodas (Vajrasana Pagoda, which is a five-pagoda cluster) as well as the Temple of True Awakening where the Pagodas housed were built in Beijing. |
| 1483~1487 | 19th~23rd year,Chenghua, Xianzong, | The layout of Confucian Temple in Qufu, Shandong, was completed in today's range and appearance. |
| 1506~1521 | Reign Period of Zhengde, Wuzong | Jichang Garden in Wuxi, Jiangsu, was built. It was famous for its "Eight-Scaled Ravine". |
| 1509 | 4th year, Zhengde, Wuzong | Wang Xianchen, a censor of the Court, dismissed from office and returned to his home town Suzhou, where he built a garden and named it "Zhuozheng Yuan" (the Humble Administrator's Garden). |
| 1519 | 14th year, Zhengde, Wuzong | The Palace of Heavenly Purity and Palace of Earthly Tranquillity in the Forbidden City of Beijing, were rebuilt. |
| 1522~1566 | Reign Period of Jiajing, Shizong | Liu Yuan, or the Lingering Garden, in Suzhou was first built. It was restored in the Qing Dynasty. |
| 1530 | 9th year, Jiajing, Shizong | Altar of Earth, Altar of the Sun and Altar of the Moon were constructed in the outskirts of Beijing. A series of sacrifices to Heaven, Earth, the Sun and the Moon in the four outskirts of the capital city were restored. Altar of Agriculture was rebuilt. |
| 1531 | 10th year, Jiajing, Shizong | Temple for Offering Sacrifices to Emperors of the Past Dynasties was built in Beijing. |
| 1534 | 13th year, Jiajing, Shizong | The Altar of Heaven and Earth in Beijing was turned into the Altar of Heaven, or the Temple of Heaven. |
| 1537 | 16th year, Jiajing, Shizong | The Hall of Mental Cultivation in the Forbidden City in Beijing was newly built. |
| 1540 | 19th year, Jiajing, Shizong | The Stone Pailou of the Ming Tombs in Changping, Beijing, was erected. |
| 1545 | 24th year, Jiajing, Shizong | The Imperial Ancestral Temple in Beijing was rebuilt. The Main Hall of the Temple of Heaven in Beijing was rebuilt. The hall which had been rectangular in plan was changed into a triple-eaved circular building, and renamed as the Hall of Prayer for Good Harvest. |
| 1559 | 38th year, Jiajing, Shizong | Being a private garden in Shanghai, Yu Yuan was built by Pan Yunduan, a retired official. The rockery there was piled up by Zhang Nanyang, a famous rockery craftsman at that time. |
| 1568 | 2nd year, Longqing, Muzong | General Qi Jiguang was appointed to garrison Jizhou near Beijing. Hence the Great Wall was restored and extended, and many more beacon towers and passes were built along the Great Wall. |
| 1573~1619 | Years of Wanli, Shenzong | Mi Wanzhong built his personal garden Shao Yuan in Beijing, which was famous for its four rarities: hill, water, flowers and rocks. |
| 1583 | 11th year, Wanli, Shenzong | Construction of Dingling Tomb (the Mausoleum of Emperor Wanli) in Changping, Beijing, started. |

| Christian era | Chinese Dynastic Years | Events or Achievements |
|---|---|---|
| 1583 | 26th year, Wanli, Shenzong | The Later Jin built Xingjingling Tombs (Tombs of Imperial Ancestors of the Qing) in Xinbin, Liaoning. The Tombs were renamed as Yongling Tombs in 1659. |
| 1615 | 48th year, Wanli, Shenzong | The Three Great Halls of the Forbidden City in Beijing were rebuilt. |
| 1629 | 2nd year, Chongzhen, Sizong | The Later Jin built Fuling Tomb (Tomb of Nurhachi, Emperor Taizu of the Qing) in Shenyang, Liaoning. |
| 1634 | 7th year, Chongzhen, Sizong | Yuan ye, a treatise on Chinese gardens written by Ji Cheng, was published. |
| 1640 | 13th year, Chongzhen, Sizong | The Qing Court built Dugong Hall (the Hall of Great Power) of the Imperial Palace in Shenyang. |
| 1643 | 16th year, Chongzhen, Sizong | Zhaoling Tomb (Tomb of Huangtaiji, Emperor Taizong of the Qing) was first built in Shenyang, Liaoning. |
| **The Qing Dynasty** | | |
| 1645~1911 | | The traditional styles of local dwelling houses what we may catch sight of today had been formed to a great extent. |
| 17th century | Early Qing Period | Tomb of Apak Hoja (Khwaja) in Kashi, Xinjiang, was first built. The tomb underwent several renovations in later years. |
| 1644~1661 | Reign Period of Shunzhi, Shizu | The West Imperial Garden (the Three Imperial Lakes with their surroundings) was reconstructed west of the Forbidden City in Beijing. The White Dagoba was erected on the top of the hill of the Jade Flower Islet in the Northern Lake (present-day Beihai Park). |
| 1645 | 2nd year, Shunzhi, Shizu | Dalai Lama the Fifth rebuilt and extended the Potala Palace in Lhasa, Tibet. |
| 1655 | 12th year, Shunzhi, Shizu | The Palace of Heavenly Purity and Palace of Earthly Tranquillity of the Forbidden City in Beijing were rebuilt. |
| 1661 | 18th year, Shunzhi, Shizu | The Eastern Qing Tomb in Zunhua, Hebei, began to be constructed. |
| 1662~1722 | Reign Period of Kangxi, Shengzu | Chengqi Lou, a circular dwelling of the Hakkas was built in Yongding County, Fujian. |
| 1663 | 2nd year, Kangxi, Shengzu | Xiaoling Tomb (the Mausoleum of Emperor Shunzhi) was completed in the Eastern Qing Tombs in Zunhua, Hebei. |
| 1672 | 11th year, Kangxi, Shengzu | Temple of Marquis Wu Xiang in memory of Zhuge Liang was built in Chengdu, Sichuan. |
| 1677 | 16th year, Kangxi, Shengzu | The layout of Dai Miao (the Temple of Eastern Sacred Mountain) in Mount Tai, Shandong, was completed in today's scale. |
| 1680 | 19th year, Kangxi, Shengzu | Chengxin Yuan, an imperial garden at Jade Spring Hill in the western suburbs of Beijing, was built. It was renamed as Jingming Yuan, or the Garden of Light and Tranquillity, in later years. |
| 1681 | 20th year, Kangxi, Shengzu | Jingling Tomb (the Mausoleum of Emperor Kangxi) started to be constructed in the Eastern Qing Tombs in Zunhua, Hebei. |
| 1683 | 22nd year, Kangxi, Shengzu | Building complex of the Hall of Literary Glory in the Forbidden City in Beijing was rebuilt. |
| 1684 | 23rd year, Kangxi, Shengzu | Changchun Yuan, or the Enjoying-the-Spring Garden, was constructed in the western suburbs of Beijing. |
| 1689 | 28th year, Kangxi, Shengzu | Palace of Tranquil Longevity in the Forbidden City in Beijing was built. |
| 1690 | 29th year, Kangxi, Shengzu | The Hall of Supreme Harmony in the Forbidden City began to be rebuilt. The hall was completed in 1695. |
| 1703 | 42nd year, Kangxi, Shengzu | Construction of the Summer Resort at Chengde, Hebei, started. |
| 1710 | 49th year, Kangxi, Shengzu | Guan Di Miao, or the Temple of Lord Guan was rebuilt in Guan's birthplace Xiexian County, Shanxi. |
| 1718 | 57th year, Kangxi, Shengzu | Xiaodongling Tomb (the Tomb of Empress of Shunzhi) was built to the east of Xiaoling Tomb in the Eastern Qing Tombs in Zunhua, Hebei. |
| 1725 | 3rd year, Yongzheng, Shizong | Construction of Yuanming Yuan, or the Garden of Perfect Splendor, or Garden of Perfection and Brightness, started in the northwestern suburbs of Beijing. It was then extended and developed to 40 scenic spots during the period of Emperor Qianlong. |
| 1730 | 8th year, Yongzheng, Shizong | Tailing Tomb (the Mausoleum of Emperor Yongzheng) was first built in Yizhou (present-day Yixian, Hebei). The Tomb was completed in 1737. |
| 1734 | 12th year, Yongzheng, Shizong | The Board of Works promulgated Gongcheng Zuofa Zeli, or the Structural Regulations, as building codes for design and construction works. |
| 1735 | 13th year, Yongzheng, Shizong | Fragrant Hill Summer Resort for the emperor was built in the Western Hills of Beijing. |
| 1736~1796 | Reign period of Qianlong, Gaozong | Ge Yuliang, a well-known rockery craftsman, built the Huanxiu Shanzhuang (the Nestling-in-Green Mountain Villa) in Suzhou. |
| 1745 | 10th year, Qianlong, Gaozong | Fragrant Hill Summer Resort in the western hills of Beijing was extended and renamed as Jingyi Yuan (the Garden of Congenial Tranquillity). |

| Christian era | Chinese Dynastic Years | Events or Achievements |
|---|---|---|
| 1746~1748 | 11th~13th years, Qianlong, Gaozong | The Central Palatial Complex of the Imperial Palace in Shenyang was extended. Two lodges, or building compounds, were built and added to the east and west of the Central Complex. |
| 1750 | 15th year, Qianlong, Gaozong | The Pavilion of the Rain of Flowers was erected in the Forbidden City in Beijing.<br>Construction of Qingyi Yuan, or the Garden of Clear Ripples, started. It was an imperial garden including the Hill of Longevity and the Kunming Lake in the western suburbs of Beijing. It took 14 years to complete this garden. |
| 1751 | 16th year, Qianlong, Gaozong | Changchun Yuan (the Garden of Eternal Spring) and Qichun Yuan (the Garden of Blossoming Spring) were built to the east of Yuanming Yuan (the Garden of Perfect Splendor). |
| 1752 | 17th year, Qianlong, Gaozong | Roofing tiles of the Hall of Prayer for Good Harvest in the Temple of Heaven, Beijing, were rebuilt with blue glazed tiles.<br>The Imperial Palace in Shenyang was renovated. |
| 1755 | 20th year, Qianlong, Gaozong | Puning Si (Temple of Universal Tranquillity), in Chengde, Hebei, was built. Its main hall, Dacheng Ge (Pavilion of Mahayana) was built to imitate the main hall of Sangye Temple in Tibet. |
| 1764 | 29th year, Qianlong, Gaozong | Anyuan Miao Temple in Chengde, Hebei, was Built. |
| 1765 | 30th year, Qianlong, Gaozong | Song Zongyuan, a retired official, built Wangshi Yuan, or the Garden of the Master of Fishing Nets, in Suzhou. |
| 1766 | 31st year, Qianlong, | Pule Si Temple in Chengde, Hebei, was built. |
| 1767~1771 | 32nd~36th years, Qianlong, Gaozong | Temple of the Potaraka Doctrine (Putuo Zongcheng Zhi Miao) in Chengde, Hebei, was built. |
| 1774 | 39th year, Qianlong, Gaozong | Wenyuan Ge Library in the Forbidden City, Beijing, was built. |
| 1778 | 43rd year, Qianlong, Gaozong | The Western Palatial Complex of the Imperial Palace in Shenyang was built.<br>The Mosque with Su Gong Tower in Turpan, Xinjiang, was completed. |
| 1779~1780 | 44th~45th years, Qianlong, Gaozong | Temple of Sumeru Happiness and Longevity (Xu Mi Fu Shou Zhi Miao) in Chengde, Hebei, was built. |
| 1781 | 46th year, Qianlong, Gaozong | Wensu Ge Library, Yangxi Zhai Study and Jiayin Tang Hall of the Imperial Palace in Shenyang were built. |
| 1783 | 48th year, Qianlong, Gaozong | Biyong, or the Main Hall of the Imperial College (Guo Zi Jian), in Beijing was built. |
| 1784 | 49th year, Qianlong, Gaozong | Dagobas of the City of Complete Purification (Qing Jing Hua Cheng Ta) of the West Yellow Temple in Beijing were erected. |
| 18th century | | Taer Temple in Huangzhong, Qinghai, was built. |
| 1796 | 1st year, Jiaqing, Renzong | Changling Tomb (the Mausoleum of Emperor Jiaqing) of t h e Western Qing Tombs in Yixian, Hebei, was first built. It was completed eight years later. |
| 1804 | 9th year, Jiaqing, Renzong | Three Palatial Complexes with Lodges of the Central Complex of the Imperial Palace in Shenyang were renovated. |
| 1832 | 12th year, Daoguang, Renzong | Muling Tomb (the Mausoleum of Emperor Daoguang) of the Western Qing Tombs in Yixian, Hebei, was first built. It was completed four years later. |
| 1859 | 9th year, Xianfeng, Wenzong | Dingling Tomb (the Mausoleum of Emperor Xianfeng) of the Eastern Qing Tombs in Zunhua, Hebei, was first built. |
| 1860 | 10th year, Xianfeng, Wenzong | Yuanming Yuan (the Garden of Perfect Splendor) and Qingyi Yuan (the Garden of Clear Ripples) were destroyed and burnt down by the Anglo-French Allied forces. |
| 1873 | 12th year, Tongzhi, Muzong | Dingdongling Tombs (Tombs of Empress Dowagers Cixi and Ci'an) were first built in the Eastern Qing Tombs in Zunhua, Hebei. The Tombs were completed in 1879. |
| 1875 | 1st year, Guangxu, Dezong | Huiling Tomb (the Mausoleum of Emperor Tongzhi) of the Eastern Qing Tombs in Zunhua, Hebei, was built. |
| 1888 | 14th year, Guangxu, Dezong | Qingyi Yuan was rebuilt and renamed as Yihe Yuan (the Summer Palace) under Empress Dowager Cixi.<br>Jianfu Palace of Qingcheng Mountain, Sichuan, was rebuilt. |
| 1909 | 1st year, Xuantong | Chongling Tomb (the Mausoleum of Emperor Guangxu) was built in the Western Qing Tombs in Yixian, Hebei. |

**The Excellence of Ancient Chinese Architecture, Chinese Edition**
Author: Ru Jinghua and Peng Hualiang
Chief Planner: Zhou Yi
Editorial Members: Wang Boyang, Wei Ran, Wang Xuelin
Editor in Charge: Wang Boyang, Ma Yan
Photographers: Zhang Zhenguang, Wei Ran, Chen Xiaoli, Li Dongxi, Cao Yang

**The Excellence of Ancient Chinese Architecture, English Edition**
Chief Planner: Zhang Huizhen
Translators: Zang Erzhong, Cui Sigan, San Mu
Editor in Charge: Qi Linlin, Zhang Huizhen
Photographers: Zhang Zhenguang, Wei Ran, Chen Xiaoli, Li Dongxi, Cao Yang
Cover Design: Fu Jinhong
Layout Design: Xiao Jinxing



**The Excellence of Ancient Chinese Architecture**

**Palace Architecture** 宫殿建筑
**Imperial Palaces of the Last Dynasty**

**Ru Jinghua and Peng Hualiang**


Published and Distributed by China Architecture & Building Press
ISBN 978-7-112-14121-0 ( 22170 )
CIP data available on request
www.cabp.com.cn

Printed on acid-free and chlorine-free bleached paper

**Printed in China**